T0274777

AMERICA AND THE YEMENS
A Complex and Tragic Encounter

BRUCE RIEDEL

BROOKINGS INSTITUTION PRESS
Washington, D.C.

Published by Brookings Institution Press
1775 Massachusetts Avenue, NW
Washington, DC 20036
www.brookings.edu/bipress
Co-published by Rowman & Littlefield
An imprint of The Rowman & Littlefield Publishing Group, Inc.
4501 Forbes Boulevard, Suite 200, Lanham, Maryland 20706
www.rowman.com

86-90 Paul Street, London EC2A 4NE

British Library Cataloguing in Publication Information Available

Library of Congress Cataloging-in-Publication Data
ISBN 978-0-8157-4013-1 (cloth)
ISBN 978-0-8157-4014-8 (electronic)

To Elizabeth

Contents

INTRODUCTION

Yemen attracts little attention in America, even in the midst of a devastating civil war and humanitarian catastrophe. Yemen is overshadowed by the rich Gulf states, the perennial Israeli-Arab conflicts, and the danger posed by Iran. Its politics are complex, tribal, and violent, with no good guys to root for.

The war has made everything worse. The Saudis and their allies deliberately block journalists from getting access to Yemen in order to cover up the horrendous consequences of their blockade and air strikes. They don't let journalists into the Kingdom of Saudi Arabia either to do serious analytical work. They don't want stories about missile strikes on Riyadh airport discouraging foreign investors. For their part, the Houthis are verbally violently anti-American and anti-Israeli. They attribute the region's problems to America's support for Israel.

Yet America has a long history of dealing with Yemen beginning in the nineteenth century when Aden was one of the busiest seaports in the world. John F. Kennedy, Jimmy Carter, and George H. W. Bush all had crises to deal with involving the Yemens. Three presidents have now dealt with the current war in Yemen.

In Arabic, Yemen is *al-Yaman*, meaning "the land to the south," or more specifically, "the land to the south of Mecca." Yemen was one of the first countries converted to Islam, and 99 percent of Yemenis today are Muslim. The once-large Jewish community was airlifted to Israel in the late 1940s, an operation America was very much involved in, as we will see.

The city of Sana'a, the capital, is dominated by the Al Saleh Mosque, named after former president Ali Abdallah Saleh, who opened it in 2008. It is the largest mosque in the country and can host forty-four thousand worshippers. It cost $60 million and is open to non-Muslim tourists.

The north of Yemen is the highest spot on the Arabian Peninsula. It is called the Roof of Arabia and is the home of the Zaydi sect, which has dominated Yemeni politics for decades. The entire country is 208,849 square miles, almost the size of Texas. It sits athwart the Bab al-Mandab, the strait that divides Asia and Africa and links the Red Sea to the Indian Ocean.

The idea of Yemen as a united country has held an attraction for Yemenis for decades but was realized only for a few years in the 1990s and early 2000s. The country has been fractured for most of its modern history. The north has been independent since World War I; the south was a British colony until 1968 and then a satellite of the Soviet Union until 1990. The north is divided between a mountainous and harsh interior and a more settled coastal region. The south is divided many ways: there is the port city of Aden, a welter of sheikdoms around it, and then the remote east, with its big provinces of Hadhramaut and Al Mahra. The Wadi Hadhramaut is the biggest wadi, or canyon, in the peninsula, with a length of almost one hundred miles. It has nurtured a unique culture. It is also the ancestral homeland of Osama bin Laden. The east is closer to Oman than to northern Yemen. The large island of Socotra off the coast of Somalia is a unique environment, home to many exotic plants.

Sectarian religious and tribal identity matter for many Yemenis more than national identity. The Zaydi Shia in the far north are a uniquely Yemeni subculture. Yemenis are united by their fierce opposition to outsiders—Egyptians in the 1960s, Saudis today. They have waged war against outside states for generations, taking advantage of the bleak rugged interior to wear down opponents. Yemenis are Arabs and Muslims, with strong support for the Palestinian cause.

Yemen is a water-starved country where climate change is making an already difficult environment worse. There are fewer than a hundred hospitals, with one doctor for every five thousand people. Literacy is 70 percent for males and only about 30 percent for females. Many Yemenis, especially men, are addicted to a mild narcotic, qat, which unfortunately requires lots of water to grow. The qat addiction is putting the already strained water resources in greater jeopardy. There is not enough water to grow the food Yemenis need, so much food is imported. The blockade of rebel-controlled northern Yemen is responsible for the catastrophic famine in the country.

Oil was found in Yemen in the 1980s by an American company. Yemen has three trillion barrels of proven oil reserves, ranking twenty-ninth in the world. It only consumed about sixty thousand barrels per day in 2016 and uses even less now during the civil war. It is nowhere near the quantity of its oil-rich neighbors Saudi Arabia and the United Arab Emirates. Much of its income comes from the thousands of émigré workers who live in the Gulf states.

I am grateful for the support of the Brookings Institution for the research and writing of this study. I especially thank my research assistant, Israa Saber, for her help and assistance. Many others have been helpful in my research and analysis, including Michael O'Hanlon, Annelle Sheline, Mahsa Rouhi, Yasmine Farouk, Vanda Felbab-Brown, Madiha Afzal, Katherine Harvey, and the staff of the Brookings Library and Brookings Press. The Yemeni American community has also been a source of support and help, especially in trying to lobby to end American support for the blockade and the war. The late Jamal Khashoggi was a particularly valuable source of information and commentary for me and others studying the Saudi Kingdom and its politics.

Of course, any errors of fact or judgment are solely my responsibility. The Central Intelligence Agency has reviewed the manuscript to prevent any inadvertent disclosure of confidential information. All statements of fact, opinion, or analysis are those of the author and do not reflect the official positions or views of the US government. Nothing in the content shall be construed as asserting or implying US government authentication of information or endorsement of the author's views.

My wife, Elizabeth, and I have traveled many times to Arabia. This book owes much to her companionship and assistance.

Beginnings

President Rutherford B. Hayes deserves credit for beginning America's diplomatic engagement with the Yemens. The often-overlooked president sent America's first consul, James S. Williams, to Aden in March 1880. A year before that, Yemen had its first visit by an American president. Ulysses S. Grant stopped in Aden in February 1879 en route from Egypt to India as part of his postpresidency world tour.

By 1879 Aden had been a possession of the British Empire for forty years. British forces had seized the port city on the Indian Ocean from the nominal control of the Ottoman Turkish Empire in 1839. It was the first addition to the empire in the reign of Queen Victoria. After the opening of the Suez Canal, Aden was a crucial strategic point in the sea passage from the United Kingdom to India, the jewel in the crown of the British Empire. It was one of the busiest harbors in the world.

Aden has a rich history. It was a colony of the Roman Empire at its height in AD 24. The Romans called Yemen *Arabia felix*, or "happy and lucky Arabia." Later it was part of the Sassanid Persian Empire after 570. The Prophet Muhammad converted Yemen to Islam in 630. Marco Polo visited the port in 1285. The Ottoman Empire acquired Aden in 1538 and then exercised authority irregularly afterward; it tried to reseize the city during

World War I in July 1915, but the British narrowly prevailed in its defense.[1] They sent a brigade of Indian troops from Egypt to hold off the Turkish army, which had seized half the city by the end of July; the Arab revolt led by the Hashemites in 1916 then isolated the Ottoman army in Yemen.[2] The new nation of Yemen tried to take Aden from the British as well in 1922.[3]

The American consulate in Aden protected the interests of American merchant ships involved in the maritime trade in the region. In the first half of the twentieth century, Aden was the third-busiest port in the world. The consuls often traveled widely in the Indian Ocean littoral to East Africa, especially Zanzibar, and South Asia, all of which was under the control of the British Raj. Travel within the Arabian Peninsula was less frequent because of the medieval nature of the interior, the brutal weather, and the lack of any infrastructure for travel. It was a backwater in the American diplomatic service and a hardship post, very much reliant on the local British community.

The United States was also represented in nearby Oman. The sultanate of Oman had recognized the United States as early as 1832 when Andrew Jackson was president. The sultanate was a leading power in the Indian Ocean, with its influence extending from South Asia to East Africa.

Great Britain was the dominant power in the Arabian Peninsula by the end of the nineteenth century, with protectorates over Aden and southern Yemen, Oman, and much of the southern shore of the Persian Gulf, including Kuwait, Bahrain, Qatar, and the Trucial States (now the United Arab Emirates). The collapse of the Ottoman Empire at the end of World War I further consolidated the British position. The United States did not declare war on the Ottoman Empire and played a marginal role in the postwar settlement of the Middle East.

Northern Yemen declared its independence during the war. Turkish forces held on to Sana'a for the duration of the conflict but were then evacuated home. The Zaydi tribes of the north proclaimed a new monarchy, the Mutawakkil Kingdom, and claimed all South Yemen, including Aden, as well as large parts of what is now Saudi Arabia. The Zaydis are Shia Muslims and are unique to Yemen; they have different beliefs than the Shia in Iran, Lebanon, Pakistan, and other states.

Italy was the first country to formally recognize the independence of the Mutawakki Kingdom in 1926. The Fascist government of Prime Minister Benito Mussolini was eager to increase its influence in the Red Sea and to conquer Ethiopia to add to its colonies in Eritrea and Somalia. Italy sold weapons to the Yemenis.[4] In World War II the Italians bombed Aden from their bases in East Africa, and their submarines sank several ships in the harbor before the British overran the Italian East African colonies.[5] The American consul in Aden was remarkably busy in the war monitoring the sea traffic supporting the Allies' fight against the Axis powers.

MISSION TO SANA'A

The Mutawakkil imam in 1918 wrote to President Woodrow Wilson asking for American recognition of the new country, but Wilson never replied. At the end of World War II, the Yemenis reached out again. This time President Franklin Roosevelt's administration responded positively. FDR had a long-standing interest in the Middle East. In 1938 he hosted a visit to Washington by Omani sultan Said bin Taimur bin Faisal al-Bustan, the first-ever visit by an Arab head of state to the United States.[6] In 1943, at the height of the war, FDR hosted Saudi princes Faysal and Khalid at the White House for the start of the American-Saudi relationship; then in November he traveled to Tehran, Iran, for a summit with Winston Churchill and Joseph Stalin. Finally, on Valentine's Day 1945, he met with King Abdelaziz Al Saud of Saudi Arabia, or Ibn Saud as he was known, on an American cruiser, the USS *Quincy*, in Egypt to formally begin, with a summit, the relationship with the Kingdom.

Early in 1945 the American consul in Aden, Harlan B. Clark, wrote to Prince Ahmed, the imam's son, asking if the United States could send a delegation to Yemen to discuss opening relations. On February 3, 1945, the prince wrote back affirmatively. Consul Clark and a doctor then traveled overland to Sana'a to see the imam to help prepare the visit. They also saw Ahmed, who asked for US help to develop his medieval, backward kingdom.[7]

Washington moved quickly to respond to the request. President Harry Truman authorized the travel of a delegation to Sana'a to answer the imam's request and negotiate a treaty of mutual recognition. The team was headed by FDR's translator from the *Quincy*, William Eddy. Eddy was a legendary figure, born in Lebanon, a marine who had worked for the Office of Strategic Services in Algeria in 1942 to prepare for the American invasion that ousted the Vichy French government. Eddy was ambassador to Saudi Arabia. He would be joined on the trip by Consul Clark and a State Department official, Richard H. Sanger.

An American destroyer, the USS *Ernest G. Small*, delivered the small party to Hudaydah, the north's largest port, on April 8, 1946. As there were no paved roads in Yemen in 1946, it took three weeks for the party to travel by horse the one hundred miles to Sana'a, which is at an altitude of seventy-two hundred feet from the Red Sea. Eddy brought a gift: a mobile radio station to give the imam modern communications. Eddy was entranced with the country, writing in his diary that they were greeted by "friendly smiling natives" and that the women were "mostly unveiled. Much prettier than in Saudi Arabia."[8]

Eddy also noted how backward the kingdom and its leader were. The imam had never visited Hudaydah or even seen the Red Sea. There were no schools or hospitals; foreigners were prohibited from immigrating to the kingdom to keep out any hint of modernity.[9] Arriving in Sana'a, the delegation found a city divided into three sections. The largest was the Arab city of Yemeni Muslims; then there was a Turkish quarter left over from the Ottomans, and a Jewish quarter represented the fifty thousand or so Jews in Yemen. The majority of the male population and a quarter of the females chewed a mild narcotic, qat, in the afternoon, contributing to the "retarded" nature of the city.[10]

The delegation was formally received by the imam and his foreign minister, Raghib Bey, who was another holdover from the Turkish Empire. Eddy presented the imam with a letter signed by President Truman dated March 4, 1946, formally recognizing the Kingdom of Yemen as a sovereign state. Ahmed bin Yahya, eighty years old, instructed Bey to negotiate with Eddy a four-page treaty of mutual recognition, a thoroughly anodyne document usually. But in this case, it proved to be exceedingly difficult to conclude. One of the imam's sons, Prince Hussein, was against any treaty and effectively blocked the talks.

Finally, in desperation, on May 4, 1946, Eddy requested a meeting with the imam and threatened to go home without a treaty. The imam turned to his foreign minister and asked for an explanation. The Turk began to cry and resigned his position in protest over Hussein's involvement. Belatedly the document was agreed to and signed by both sides. Eddy immediately left to return to Jidda, Saudi Arabia.[11]

It was a dramatic introduction to America's relations with the independent Yemen. No embassy was set up; the American embassy in Jidda and the consul in Aden would handle any business required. The State Department estimated that only seven Americans had ever visited Yemen before 1946.[12] In September J. Rives Childs presented his credentials to the Yemeni kingdom as the US minister to Yemen. Childs was also the American ambassador to Saudi Arabia and was resident in Jidda, traveling occasionally to visit Yemen.

The Eddy mission was a portent of America's future relations with the Yemens. It was largely a derivative of America's relationship with Saudi Arabia. Saudi Arabia, then larger in size but not population, has immense repositories of oil. It is a world power in the energy field. Eddy personally embodied America's ties to the Kingdom. Yemen was a decidedly secondary priority for America and a secondary priority for Eddy. Washington all too often saw developments in Sana'a and Aden through Riyadh's eyes and interests.

An exception came in 1949. The creation of Israel and the subsequent war between Israel and the Arab states significantly worsened the plight of Yemen's Jewish community. Imam Yahya agreed that the Jews could leave Yemen to go to Israel in return for their property. American Jews, with Truman's support, set up a fund to pay to fly the Yemeni Jews to Israel. Operation Magic Carpet or Operation On Wings of Eagles followed. Forty-seven thousand Jews from the north walked to Aden, where they joined another fifteen hundred from the south and two thousand from Saudi Arabia. The Americans hired Alaska Airlines to fly the 380 flights to carry the Jews to Israel. The planes flew from Asmara in Ethiopia to Aden, then to Tel Aviv, and finally to Cyprus to overnight. The British in Aden helped facilitate the operation, which lasted ten months.[13]

1962: JFK's Yemen Crisis

A legation was opened in Taiz in Yemen in March 1959 in the closing months of Dwight David Eisenhower's administration. Not a full embassy, the legation did mark a formal American diplomatic post in the kingdom. It was elevated to the status of an embassy by President John F. Kennedy in January 1963 and moved to Sana'a in 1966. Kennedy would be the first American president to confront a serious international crisis in Yemen, coming virtually at the same time as he faced the Cuban Missile Crisis with the Soviet Union and the Chinese invasion of India in the autumn of 1962.

In the late 1950s and early 1960s, the Mutawakkil Kingdom of Yemen was increasingly caught up in the political turmoil sweeping the Middle East. At the center of the turmoil was

Egyptian president Gamal abd al-Nasser. Nasser had led Egypt's own revolution in 1952, which deposed its monarchy. He set up a progressive nationalist regime that threw out the British, nationalized the Suez Canal, and fought Israel, Great Britain, and France in 1956. He was the spokesman for pan-Arabism, the notion that there should be a single united Arab state from Morocco to Oman. In 1958 Syria united with Egypt to form the United Arab Republic (UAR), and the dream of pan-Arabism seemed to be within reach.

The UAR also aligned itself with the Soviet Union and purchased arms from the Soviets. This injected the Cold War into the region. Eisenhower promised in 1957 to aid any country under threat from communism and in 1958, after the UAR merger, sent troops to Lebanon to prevent a Nasserist takeover of the country.[14]

Kennedy came into office determined to deal with Arab nationalism as a phenomenon America had to work with, not fight. As a senator he had been the first to call for Algerian independence and for the United States to cease backing the French army trying to repress the independence movement. Kennedy in office reached out to Nasser and engaged him in a long series of letters about the region, trying to develop a useful dialogue.

The Yemeni monarchy tried to appease Nasser by affiliating the country with the UAR in an entity called the United Arab States (UAS). It also invited Egypt and Russia to set up training programs for its army. The UAS collapsed in 1961 when Syria left the bloc and regained its independence. Egypt withdrew its advisors from Yemen, but the Soviets remained. Nasser began plotting to depose the monarchy with the goal of securing a foothold on the Arabian Peninsula that could be a base to overthrow the Saudi monarchy and seize Aden from the British.

On September 19, 1962, Imam Ahmed, the man who invited Eddy to Sana'a, died. He had ruled since his father's death in 1948. Ahmed was nicknamed al-Djinn, or the devil: he killed four of his nine brothers and kept a harem of thirty-five women. The thirty-six-year-old Muhammad al-Badr ascended to the throne. A week later the army attacked the royal palace and created the Yemen Arab Republic (YAR). Egypt immediately recognized the new state. Badr loyalists fought back in the countryside.

Egypt and Russia moved quickly to back the new YAR. The principal driver of the Egyptian intervention was Anwar Sadat, Nasser's ultimate successor, who argued it was a way to restore the momentum toward Arab unity after the Syrian withdrawal from the UAR. It would also offer a base for operations against Saudi Arabia and Aden. Sadat arrived in Sana'a three days after the coup to coordinate Egyptian support. The Egyptian intervention was code-named Operation 9000.[15]

The Soviets were equally swift to move. They recognized the new Yemeni government on October 1, 1962, the first non-Arab state to do so. They already had a substantial presence in the country. In addition to providing military advisers, the Soviets had built a modern harbor and port infrastructure in Hudaydah in the late 1950s, which soon became the gateway for Egyptian troops to enter the country. Moscow's ally, Communist China, had built the highway linking Hudaydah to Sana'a. In the first year of the war, Egypt used eighteen ships to make 122 deliveries of supplies to Yemen.

But the immediate requirement was an airlift of troops, weapons, and other material to Sana'a to bolster the republicans against the counterrevolutionary royalist forces. On September 26, 1962, Nasser and Sadat asked Russia to help. Nikita Khrushchev and the Soviets responded by sending ten large Antonov An-12 heavy-lift aircraft to Egypt with Russian crews. The first flight arrived in Sana'a on September 30.

Moscow's support went beyond the airlift. Beginning in late October (at the climax of the Cuban Missile Crisis), Soviet Tupolev TU-16 twin-engine bombers began bombing royalist targets along the Saudi-Yemeni border. The TU-16s were also flown by Russian crews. The operation was code-named Mubarak after Husni Mubarak (Sadat's successor), who was the nominal Egyptian commander of the TU-16 squadron. In early October four Russian advisors were captured by the royalists near the city of Marib; the royalists sent them to Aden for the British, who then repatriated them to Moscow.

Kennedy was closely monitoring the situation. The Central Intelligence Agency (CIA) provided him with a daily written summary of its top-secret intelligence, called the President's Intelligence Checklist (PICKL). The PICKLs for the fall of 1962 are available on the CIA's declassified website, where they are arranged by date. In the fall of 1962, especially late September and October, three stories dominated the book: Cuba, India, and Yemen. The day after the coup, the CIA reported that Badr's uncle Hasan was rallying the northern Zaydi Shia tribes along the Saudi border to fight to restore the monarchy. The next day it identified the leader of the coup as Brigadier General Abdallah al-Sallal, the commander of the imam's bodyguards. The brief said Cairo was "delighted" over the coup and was complicit in its occurrence. The agency reported that Sallal and other senior coup plotters were members of the Free Yemeni Movement, which Egypt backed.

Kennedy was told by the intelligence analysts on October 2, 1962, that "a civil war is shaping up with direct backing from the UAR and from Saudi Arabia" for the opposing sides. Two Saudi pilots then defected to Egypt with their US-made aircraft, which were bringing arms to the royalists. It emerged that Badr had not died in the coup attempt but had successfully fled Sana'a to join the royalists in their camps in Saudi Arabia. Jordan was also providing aid to the royalists. On October 6, 1962, the PICKL reported, "The struggle in Yemen is becoming international," and five days later it told Kennedy, "Soviet pilots are now flying supplies and equipment in from Cairo in AN-12 transports."

The president was urged by Saudi Arabia and Jordan, as well as the British, to back the royalists and not recognize the new government. The CIA reported King Hussein was pressing both

Washington and Riyadh to "intervene in force in Yemen before it is too late." Hussein warned that a revolution in Saudi Arabia "could all too easily be ignited by an adventure from Yemen." By October 31, the CIA estimated Egypt had four thousand troops in country. That would grow to thirty thousand by March 1963. Jordan had moved a battalion of its army to Saudi Arabia to help the royalists.

Saudi crown prince Faysal was in New York for the annual UN General Assembly meeting in October. Faysal pressed Kennedy to conduct a show of force in the Red Sea to halt Egyptian arms and troops from going to Hudaydah. Kennedy demurred from intervening. On October 5, 1962, he met with the prince in the White House, including a private one-on-one meeting in the family quarters of the building, a highly unusual honor for a foreign visitor. They agreed that the United States would publicly reaffirm its commitment to preserve the independence and integrity of Saudi Arabia and would step up port visits by the US Navy to Saudi ports and increase training for Saudi personnel in the Royal Saudi Air Force.[16]

But Kennedy also made clear to the crown prince that he believed the most serious threat to the survival of the House of Saud came from within the country. Unless Saudi Arabia took steps to modernize, Kennedy believed, the monarchy was doomed. In the private one-on-one, Faysal promised to abolish slavery in Saudi Arabia, begin women's education, and end arbitrary arrest and confinement. It was an extraordinary and unique moment in America's relationship with the Kingdom, the only time an American president has intervened successfully in its internal affairs.[17]

Faysal made a deep impression on the president, unlike his incompetent brother King Saud, whom Faysal would oust in November 1964 with the Royal Guards, literally at sword point.[18] Saud moved to Cairo at first and then went into exile in Greece. Kennedy found Faysal to be trustworthy and enlightened. He was also a profoundly pious man.

At the height of the Cold War, the Soviet Union led by Nikita Khrushchev was directly intervening in a civil war in Yemen that threatened the survival of the Kingdom of Saudi Arabia, America's oldest partner in the Arab world. Unlike in Cuba, the Soviets in Yemen, with their Egyptian partners, did not back down but rather escalated the conflict.

The stakes were potentially enormous. If Yemen fell completely into the hands of Nasser and Khrushchev, then the Egyptians and Russians would have a base to subvert the kingdoms of the Arabian Peninsula, most importantly Saudi Arabia, with the largest deposits of oil in the world. Lesser sheikdoms like Kuwait would also be at risk; so would Jordan. The balance of power not just in the region but in the world would tilt toward Moscow.

Concerned about the likely revolutionary spillover from Yemen to Aden, the British set up a secret organization, run out of 21A Sloane Street in London, to help arm and train the royalists.[19] The British would recruit mercenaries, many from Belgium and France, with experience in insurgency to assist the royalists, Saudis, and Jordanians in fighting the republicans, Egyptians, and Soviets.

Israel, which had its own differences with Nasser, joined in the clandestine campaign. The royalists reached out to Israeli diplomats in Europe. Badr sent a representative to Tel Aviv to ask the Israeli secret intelligence service, the Mossad, for help. The Mossad sent an operations officer to Yemen to coordinate on the ground with the royalists. In the next few years, Israeli Air Force Boeing C97 Stratofreighters flew round-trip from Tel Nof airbase over the Saudi Kingdom to drop supplies of weapons to the royalists with Saudi approval and knowledge. Nahum Admoni was Mossad's officer in charge of Operation Rotev (meaning "gravy"); he would go on to become its director in the 1980s.[20] His predecessor in the 1960s met with his Saudi counterpart at the Dorchester Hotel in London to coordinate their operations.[21]

In November 1962, the CIA told Kennedy, "All our evidence indicates that the UAR, Saudi Arabia and Jordan are getting themselves more and more deeply embroiled in the Yemen war" and informed him that several hundred Soviet soldiers were also on the ground. "Soviet involvement, directly and through the UAR, is growing." But Kennedy kept America out of the war, ultimately recognizing the republican government of the YAR, which irritated Faysal and Hussein. The CIA warned the president that both Saudi Arabia and Jordan were highly vulnerable to their own revolutionaries. Hussein told the US ambassador in Amman on November 19, 1962, "I wonder who will be next, King Saud or me?"

Both kingdoms were weak. The Saudis could barely summon five thousand combat-ready troops. The Royal Saudi Air Force had to be confined to the ground because of repeated defections of planes and pilots to Egypt. The Royal Jordanian Air Force, Hussein's pride and joy, sent six fighters to Saudi Arabia to help defend the kingdom; the squadron commander and two aircraft defected to Egypt.

Kennedy did send F-100 Super Sabre aircraft to Saudi Arabia in 1963 in a vivid show of US support for the defense of the Kingdom. By then there were almost daily Egyptian airstrikes at royalist bases on the border, often in Saudi territory. Operation Hardsurface, the first-ever deployment of American combat forces to the Arabian Peninsula, began in July 1963.[22] It ended shortly before Kennedy's assassination in Dallas, Texas, in November.

JFK handled the Yemen crisis coolly and prudently. He judged, based on the CIA's reporting, that the royalists had more than enough help from the Saudis, Jordanians, British, and Israelis; they did not need American covert assistance as well. He was aware that the royalists were medieval in their worldview, not agents of change. He further realized that the Saudi monarchy was also backward and that the biggest threat to its survival was internal, not Egypt. He found an ally in Faysal, who also wanted to modernize the Kingdom for its own survival. He kept his line of communication with Nasser open and sent high-level representatives to Cairo to meet with the Egyptians. Finally, he recognized the YAR and kept an embassy in Sana'a to provide real-time, on-the-ground situation reports.

The war in Yemen escalated further on President Lyndon Johnson's watch. By 1966 seventy thousand Egyptian soldiers in Yemen were bogged down in a quagmire that was bankrupting Cairo. Sadat continued to push to win the war. One-third of the Egyptian army (and the best of it) was in Yemen when the Six-Day War broke out with Israel in June 1967.[23] Israeli experts acknowledge part of the reason for Israel's stunning success against Egypt was the distraction of Yemen. Yossi Alpher, who handled the Israel Defense Force's role in Rotev, said later, "We learned from prisoners we captured in the Sinai just how much the events in Yemen negatively impacted the mood and readiness of the Egyptian army."[24] The Yemen government broke relations with the United States on June 7, 1967, to protest Johnson's support for Israel.

The defeat in the Sinai in June led to the end of Egypt's intervention in Yemen. Faysal and Nasser reached an agreement shortly after the war to end support to the warring parties, and the Egyptians evacuated Yemen. It is estimated that twenty-five thousand Egyptian soldiers died in the quagmire, twice as many as died in the June 1967 war. Sallal was ousted in a coup shortly afterward, and a new republican government came to power in Sana'a. Sallal went into exile in Iraq.[25] The royalists besieged the capital in November 1967, but the republicans held out, and the siege lifted in February 1968. A final cease-fire ended the civil war in 1970 with a republic still in place. By then the United States was completely consumed with the war in Vietnam.

AMERICA'S BRIEF MOMENT IN ADEN

The British were right to worry that Aden would be the next target after Egypt and Russia intervened in the north. By 1967 a vicious three-way civil war was underway in the south. The British were trying to prop up the traditional tribal elites as they promised independence. The rebel forces were divided between the Front for the Liberation of South Yemen (FLOSY) and the National Liberation Front (NLF). Egypt backed FLOSY, and Russia backed the NLF.

A rebellion against the British began in 1964. It quickly gained steam. There were 36 violent incidents in 1964, 286 in 1965, 480 in 1966, and 2,908 in 1967.[26] With the Suez Canal closed, the strategic importance of Aden was diminished, and London decided to get out. The British appealed to the United Nations to help secure a cease-fire and an orderly transition of power.

In the spring of 1967, the UN General Assembly created a mission to go to Aden and try to arrange the end of hostilities. Venezuela, Afghanistan, and Mali provided representatives to lead the mission; my father, Milton Riedel, was its adminis-trative officer. Leaving from New York they went to London, Cairo, Jidda, and finally Aden. They arrived in Aden on April 2, 1967. The rebels refused to meet with them. The United Nations refused to meet with the British-supported tribal leaders. So the mission members stayed in their hotel, the Seaview, on the coast, surrounded by British troops from the Royal Northumberland Fusiliers. It was a dangerous and useless mission. My dad was glad to get out alive when they departed on April 7.

The British evacuated the city in November 1967, and the NLF quickly emerged as the victor in the struggle, creating the People's Democratic Republic of Yemen (PDRY) on November 29, 1967. The United States still had a consulate in Aden, as it had since 1880. One of the new officers in the region was a young CIA operations officer, Robert C. Ames. Ames, unusually, had exceptional Arabic skills, so he had a particularly important role in translating.

When Ames arrived in October 1967, he was unaccompanied. His wife and four children remained in the United States because of instability in the region. Aden was a war zone, and attacks on civilian targets were frequent. After the British withdrawal, the country returned quickly to normal. Ames's family joined him in his host country. By their own account, they loved visiting Aden. They could go to the market in the heart of old Aden formed in the crater of an extinct volcano. They also traveled to the far east of southern Yemen, the province of Hadhramaut.

Ames befriended Abd al-Fattah Ismail, a founding member of the NLF trained in Moscow by the Soviets to create a Communist state. Ismail wanted contact with Washington, and Ames became his interlocuter, probably because Ames was fluent in Arabic and sympathetic to the Arab nationalist cause. It was a big boost to Ames's career to have a contact at the top of the PDRY. In late 1968 he became a senior CIA manager at a very young age. By then Ismail had been arrested in an internal coup in the government. He led his coup in 1969 and was the leader of the PDRY until his death in a firefight in January 1986.

The American interlude in the only Communist country in the Arab world was bound to end. In October 1969, the PDRY broke relations with the United States. Ames lost his ability to travel to Aden. Eight years later Ames would be my first guru and friend in the CIA. Tragically he was killed in the bombing of the US Embassy in Beirut on April 18, 1983. He is buried in Arlington National Cemetery.[27]

In October 1973, the Egyptian navy, with PDRY support, blockaded the strait between the Red Sea and the Indian Ocean to traffic bound for Israel. The Bab al-Mandab, or Gate of Tears, is a twenty-mile-wide waterway between Yemen and Eritrea, with an island, Perim, in the middle, which belongs to South Yemen. The blockade was a fitting codicil to Egypt's intervention in Yemen. Two Egyptian destroyers and two submarines denied Israel oil from its then partner Iran. Iran had been exporting eighteen million tons of oil annually to Israel via the Bab al-Mandab. The blockade was one of the pressure points that eventually compelled Israel to give back the Sinai.

Ali Abdallah Saleh and Dancing Snakes

One individual dominated Yemen's politics from the mid-1970s to his violent death in 2017. Ali Abdallah Saleh often said ruling Yemen was like dancing on the heads of snakes. Every American president from James Carter to Donald Trump dealt with Saleh, often dancing through Yemen's deadly politics to try to get him to do what the United States wanted. Saleh proved elusive at best.

North Yemen spent the first years of the 1970s recovering from the civil war of the 1960s. The republican forces had won the civil war largely through the collective exhaustion of all the belligerents. The Saudis were much less interested in the country after the departure of the Egyptians and the Russians. King Faysal's attention was more focused on the rapid development of the Saudi economy after the 1973 Arab-Israeli conflict. His assassination two years later put his brother Khalid on the throne; Khalid was also focused inward.

The United States reopened relations with the north in July 1972 after a visit to Sana'a by Secretary of State William Rogers. Rogers was not close to President Richard Nixon and his national security advisor Henry Kissinger. The resumption of relations did not auger a major investment of American diplomacy in sleepy Sana'a. That would come under Jimmy Carter.

DEALING WITH THE PDRY

Washington was much more focused on the south. The People's Democratic Republic of Yemen (PDRY), with its government headquartered in Aden, was the only Communist state in the Arab world. For Nixon and Kissinger, it was a base for Soviet subversion of the region against US allies, like Saudi Arabia and Oman. This threatened the stability of the world's oil resources. It also threatened North Yemen.

The north and south fought a brief war in 1972. The war was precipitated by a Saudi plot to destabilize the south in early 1972. Saudi-backed rebels moved into eastern South Yemen. Prime Minister Ali Nasir Muhammad survived an assassination plot by the rebels in May. In September, the north attacked the south on the tenth anniversary of the coup that ousted the monarchy in the north. The north got assistance and support from Saudi Arabia, Jordan, Iran, the United Kingdom, and the United States. The south got help from the Soviets, Iraq, Libya, and Cuba. This short, inconclusive war ended after twenty-three days with a cease-fire.

A much more serious conflict was underway in neighboring Oman. Sultan Said bin Taimur deliberately kept Oman isolated and medieval to forestall threats to his authority. The country was desperately poor and backward. The British managed its foreign and defense policy. The westernmost province of the sultanate, Dhofar, was the private reserve of the sultan and the most backward region. The sultan preferred to stay in Salalah, Dhofar's capital, rather than Muscat, where he felt he had many enemies.

In 1962 a local tribal leader revolted in Dhofar and was backed by the Saudis, who were long-standing enemies of the sultan. They were rivals for territory in southwestern Arabia and divided on religious grounds; the Saudis are Wahhabi Muslims, whereas the Omanis are Ibadi Muslims, a unique form of

Islam found only in Oman. The weak Omani military fought a low-intensity war against the Dhofari rebels with British help.

In the late 1960s the rebellion was radicalized. The British withdrawal from Aden and the creation of the PDRY created a new source of aid in place of the Saudis. The movement renamed itself the Popular Front for the Liberation of the Occupied Arabian Gulf, with the goal of ousting all the British protectorates in the Persian Gulf from Oman to Kuwait. The PDRY provided bases in the south for the rebels, where they also got assistance from Russia, China, East Germany, and Cuba. The insurgents overran much of Dhofar outside Salalah. Washington saw the rebellion as the tip of the spear of Soviet subversion of the Arabian Peninsula. That got the attention of Nixon and Kissinger.

Robert Ames visited Oman from Aden in October 1967. He flew to Salalah with the consul general from Aden. The sultan lived in a mud palace. Ames wrote to his wife, "This is one of the most inaccessible kingdoms" in the world. After their audience with the sultan, Ames and the consul were given a tour of the gardens by his twenty-seven-year-old son, Qaboos bin Said. He confided to Ames that he was under virtual house arrest by his father and was allowed only a handful of books. A graduate of Sandhurst, Britain's military academy, Qaboos would be placed on the throne three years later on July 23, 1970, in a coup orchestrated by the British, who came to believe the medieval monarchy needed new blood to survive.

The Communist rebellion in Dhofar got more entrenched as the PDRY gave it support and sanctuary across the border. The new sultan announced an amnesty for insurgents willing to give up the war and brought in more British advisers for his army. He instituted comprehensive reforms to modernize the country.

Qaboos also turned to another ally, Iran, for troops. Nixon encouraged the alliance; he and Kissinger saw Iran as the main pillar of the defense of the Gulf in the 1970s. A brigade of Iranian imperial troops arrived in 1973. It expanded to the Imperial

Iranian Task Force, numbering four thousand troops equipped with helicopters. King Hussein and Jordan provided a company of military engineers to help the shah and the sultan. The Iranian expeditionary force lost two hundred killed, but it tilted the balance.[1]

Qaboos visited Washington in January 1975, his first and only state visit to America, to thank the United States for its help against the PDRY. President Gerald Ford, Kissinger, and National Security Advisor Brent Scowcroft met with the sultan in the Oval Office. Qaboos told Ford that the South Yemenis were training about five hundred Dhofaris a year in camps in Aden with assistance from East Germany's secret intelligence service. Kissinger characterized the South Yemeni Communists as "a nasty bunch." When Qaboos asked for sniper scopes, Scowcroft promised to get them for the Omani army.[2]

The driving force behind South Yemen's aggressive policy to radicalize Oman and the rest of the Gulf in the 1970s was Abd al-Fattah Ismail, Ames's contact. After briefly being in exile in 1968, he returned in 1969 to be the head of the Communist Party in the PDRY. He pushed a very extreme revolutionary line. But it was unsuccessful; no other state fell to the revolution. In 1980 he resigned his position and left for Moscow for medical treatment. He would return to Aden five years later.

THE RISE OF SALEH

Ali Abdallah Saleh was a self-made man. He was born March 21, 1942, to a poor Zaydi family outside Sana'a. He joined the Yemeni army in 1958 as an infantryman and was admitted to the military academy two years later. In 1963 he graduated as a lieutenant. He backed the 1962 coup that toppled the monarchy and fought in the civil war against the royalists. In 1970 he went to Iraq for training at the Iraqi Higher Command and Staff School, returning in 1971 as a lieutenant colonel. He was twice jailed by Imam Yahya for subversion but was released on good behavior and stayed in the army. His time in Iraq turned him into a supporter of republicanism. In 1977 he was appointed military governor of Taiz, the former royal capital of the country.[3]

The early and mid-1970s were an era of intense political instability in the Yemen Arab Republic. Coups, assassinations, and plots consumed the victors of the civil war of the 1960s. With the departure of the Egyptians, Abdallah al-Sallal was ousted in a coup led by Abdul Rahman Yahya al-Eryani. Sallal was in Iraq when the coup took place and went into exile in Egypt.[4] Eryani was a longtime republican agitator who had been sentenced to beheading by the monarchy only to be saved at the last minute by Imam Yahya in an act of clemency. He was an opponent of relying on the Egyptians in the civil war and was given the job of minister for religious endowments to keep him out of the decision making during the war. He presided over the formal end of the war in 1970 and the restoration of diplomatic ties with Saudi Arabia in the same year. The United States restored relations in 1972. He was ousted in another coup in 1974 and spent the rest of his life in exile in Damascus, Syria.

Ibrahim al-Hamdi took power on June 13, 1974. He had fought in the civil war as a commando and became deputy prime minister for internal affairs in 1972. The economy boomed on his watch, thanks to the oil boom in the Gulf states, and he expressed interest in unification with South Yemen. He was scheduled to travel to Aden to negotiate a unity agreement when he was assassinated in the home of Ahmad al-Ghashmi, reportedly with Saudi assistance, on October 11, 1977.[5]

Ghashmi was dead within eight months. He was assassinated while receiving a delegation from the PDRY. One of the delegates carried a briefcase with a bomb inside and blew up himself, Ghashmi, and several others on June 24, 1978. The briefcase was sent by the then South Yemeni leader Salim Rubai Ali, who was killed in a coup in Aden three days later.

Ali Abdallah Saleh took power in the wake of the bombing. He faced his own crisis, a war with the south, less than a year later. The war was the outcome of the intense rivalry in Aden between hard-liners led by Ismail and more moderate Communists led by Salim Rubai Ali. With Ali's death, the radicals determined it was time to unify Yemen by force. On February 24, 1979, in response to a raid from the north probably not authorized by Saleh, the PDRY mounted a full-scale invasion across the border.

South Yemen had air superiority thanks to assistance from Russia and East Germany. Eight hundred Cuban troops assisted the south. The Soviets had one thousand advisers and experts in the south. Southern tanks were on the verge of seizing Taiz, which would have been a staggering blow to Saleh. On March 8, the southern air force bombed Sana'a; two days later they raided Hudaydah. Saleh appealed to Washington, Baghdad, and Riyadh for help.

President Jimmy Carter responded decisively. It was a critical moment for Carter: the shah had just fled Tehran, and the president was heading for Cairo to try to finish the Egyptian-Israeli peace deal. Carter and his national security advisor, Zbigniew Brzezinski, saw the PDRY offensive as a Soviet and Cuban test of the president's resolve to defend America's allies in the Middle East. Eighteen F-5 jet fighters were dispatched to fight the PDRY air force. Since Yemen had no pilots trained on the F-5, Carter got Taiwan to send eighty pilots and air crews to operate and maintain them. Saudi Arabia agreed to pay for the jets and crews as well as tanks, artillery, and other equipment for the north, which would amount to $300 million. Iraqi sent air defense crews to help protect Sana'a. The US Navy made a show of force in the Red Sea, deploying several warships.[6]

Iraq also used its political influence to secure a cease-fire. On March 20, 1979, in Kuwait, the two sides signed a cease-fire and promised to unify peacefully. That did not happen, but the Arab intervention to end the crisis and the rush of American aid to the north undermined the strength of the radicals in Aden. In 1980 Abd al-Fattah Ismail went into voluntary exile in Moscow.

The Kuwait agreement and the aid from outside, including from Carter and Saddam Hussein, gave Saleh a tremendous boost. He would then bring stability and order to the country after two decades of war, assassinations, coups, and intrigue. He famously said that ruling Yemen was like dancing on the heads of snakes because its politics were split by tribal enmities, religious differences, and geography. Moreover, outside parties, especially the Saudis, meddled endlessly in the north's politics.

The first years of Saleh's more than three decades in power were tumultuous ones in the Middle East. Anwar Sadat traveled to Jerusalem in November 1977 and then signed the Egyptian-Israeli peace treaty with Menachem Begin in early 1979. The treaty was the work of President Carter, who devoted enormous time and attention, as well as political capital, to getting it done. Like almost all the Arab states, except Oman, Yemen broke diplomatic relations with Egypt after the treaty was signed, and Saleh joined in the boycott of Sadat that would continue until his assassination in October 1981 by armed militants angry about the peace with Israel.

In Iran, the shah was toppled from power in 1979, and the American diplomats at the embassy in Tehran were held prisoner by the Islamic radicals who had overthrown the shah. Saleh, a republican, was hostile to Ayatollah Ruhollah Khomeini's Islamic Republic and its efforts to export its revolution to other states, especially those with Shia majorities. Yemen supported Iraq in September 1980 when it invaded Iran to try to topple Khomeini. Saleh's years in Iraq undoubtedly contributed to his inclination to back Saddam Hussein. Oman was even more supportive given the shah's role in defeating the Dhofar rebellion. Sultan Qaboos offered to let the Iraqi air force bomb Iranian targets like Bandar Abbas from Omani airfields. If the Iraqis had done so, the war would have widened quickly. Carter weighed in with the sultan, and Oman retracted the offer.[7]

Yemen and Saleh would support Iraq and Saddam throughout the eight long years of the Iran-Iraq War. Yemeni "volunteers" fought with the Iraqis. The war was the longest conventional conflict in the world since the Korean War. At least five hundred thousand Iranians and perhaps three hundred thousand Iraqis died.[8]

Saleh also moved closer to the Soviets, Iraq's patron, and signed a treaty of friendship and cooperation with Russia in 1984. Saleh traveled to Moscow to sign the treaty, which also had the virtue of calming relations with the PDRY, which was very dependent on Soviet aid.[9]

Many years later Carter would go to Yemen and say it was the most fascinating country he had ever visited. He even tried qat, the mild narcotic most Yemenis chew. Carter's decisive stance in 1979 made Saleh's survival possible.[10]

Relations with Ronald Reagan were cordial but not close. The Reagan administration was plagued by Iranian-backed terrorism and by a series of grave self-imposed political mistakes in its Middle East policy. It backed Israel's disastrous invasion of Lebanon in 1982, which led to the bombing of the US Marine Corps barracks at the Beirut airport and the rise of the military Shia terrorist group Hezbollah, bankrolled by Iran. It pursued the stupid policy of trading arms for hostages with Iran known as Iran Contra, again at Israel's urging, which almost led to Reagan's impeachment. Finally, it engaged in an unofficial naval war with Iran in 1988 that helped end the Iran-Iraq War.

Saleh did support Reagan's clandestine war in Afghanistan. Thousands of Yemeni men volunteered to fight with the Afghan mujahedin against the Soviet Union. Saleh encouraged them to go and supported clerics who preached in favor of the war and the Arab Afghans fighting there. The most famous of course was Osama bin Laden, the son of a Yemeni from the Hadhramaut who emigrated to Saudi Arabia and made a fortune in the construction business. Bin Laden favored Yemenis for his bodyguards because of their loyalty and proficiency with weapons.[11]

In the midst of the Iran-Iraq War, South Yemen underwent a civil war starting on January 13, 1986, pitting the factions of the Communist Party against each other. Ismail had returned to Aden from Moscow in 1985. He had been succeeded in running the south by Ali Nasir Muhammad, who backed away from supporting Marxist rebels in other states and tried to work with Saleh to keep the border peaceful.

The war began with a firefight as the party politburo was meeting. Ismail survived the firefight but was killed a few days later. The battle ended twelve days later with the ouster of Nasir from power and his replacement with a follower of Ismail, Ali Salem al-Beidh. Around ten thousand people died in the intense combat, and Nasir and sixty thousand southerners fled to North Yemen and exile.

It was the beginning of the end for the PDRY. Soviet aid began to diminish as the Soviets struggled to keep their economy going along with meeting the high costs of the Cold War and the quagmire in Afghanistan, which they had jumped into in 1979. Without Russian financial aid, the PDRY was going broke.

In February 1989 Saleh joined with Iraq, Jordan, and Egypt in forming the Arab Cooperation Council after the cease-fire ended the Iran-Iraq War. This was intended to give the four states added political leverage in dealing with Saudi Arabia and the Gulf states, which had earlier created the Gulf Cooperation Council to deter Iran. In practice, the move indicated Saleh's steady movement toward Saddam Hussein and Baghdad. In 1989 Yemen was elected as one of the ten nonpermanent members of the United Nations Security Council starting in 1990, enhancing its importance on the global stage.

Osama bin Laden returned from Afghanistan and Pakistan in 1989, eager to lead a new jihad against the Soviets and communism in his homeland. He approached the head of Saudi intelligence, Prince Turki bin Faysal, with the idea. Turki turned him down; the Saudis did not want a jihadist army on their border. Bin Laden went ahead and began recruiting jihadists in the south to fight the PDRY.[12]

1990: THE YEAR OF DECISION

President Ali Abdallah Saleh made his first visit to Washington in January 1990. President George H. W. Bush hosted him for a state visit and meetings with his administration. Bush was the first American president that Saleh had met with in person. The two had first met in Yemen in April 1986 when then vice president Bush traveled to Saudi Arabia, Bahrain, Oman, and Yemen. Bush was there to inaugurate a new American-built oil refinery. The Texas-based Hunt Oil Company was producing oil in fields around the city of Marib in eastern North Yemen, engendering the country's new economic bonanza. Bush was greeted by eager crowds chanting "USA, USA." Bush remains the most senior American official to ever visit Yemen.[13] He was also the first president I worked for directly on the staff of the National Security Council after July 1991.

The state visit went well. Saleh met with Bush in the Oval Office and spent time on the Hill with interested senators and representatives. In the private Oval Office meeting, Bush thanked Saleh for allowing American Jews to visit the small community of Yemeni Jews who had not taken the Magic Carpet to Israel in 1949.[14] Saleh also visited New York, San Francisco, and Dallas. By all accounts, the visit went well. The good feelings would not last the year.

The previous month Saleh had signed a treaty for unification of the two Yemens with South Yemeni president Ali Salem al-Beidh. The PDRY was now completely broke, communism was in disarray, and the Union of Soviet Socialist Republics was collapsing. The unification of the two countries was immensely popular in both. The south was geographically bigger, but 80 percent of the population of the new Republic of Yemen was in the north, most of them Zaydi Shias. The north had a population of eleven million, the south two and a half million. Iraq had encouraged the unification; Saddam wanted a larger Yemen on Saudi Arabia's southern border.[15] The Saudis were not eager for a bigger Yemen.

Unification occurred on May 22, 1990; Saleh became president and Beidh vice president. Saleh had achieved the dream of every northern leader going back over a century.[16] Bush sent his congratulations to Saleh. Unification was ephemeral in some ways. The two militaries remained separate. Communists governed in most of the south, paying lip service to the Saleh government and facing armed resistance from bin Laden's jihadis.

Iraq was also broke by 1990. The war with Iran had cost a fortune; the collective economic cost was over $1 trillion. Iraq had survived only by borrowing tens of billions from Kuwait, Saudi Arabia, and the United Arab Emirates.[17] In July 1990 Saddam demanded that the loans be turned into gifts and that Kuwait and the UAE hand over more money. His argument was that Iraq had saved the Gulf Arabs from the Iranians and now they needed to pay back the Iraqi people. Saddam moved eight divisions of the Iraqi elite Republican Guard to the border with Kuwait. On August 2, 1990, they invaded and swiftly conquered the small emirate. Bush immediately came to the aid of the exiled Kuwaiti royal family in Saudi Arabia. Tens of thousands of American troops were rapidly deployed to the kingdom along with troops from Great Britain, France, and more than two dozen countries.

Yemenis were sympathetic with Iraq. They had their own grievances with the wealthy and often imperious Saudis. Saleh had a long-standing relationship with Iraq going back to his training in Baghdad. By 1990 he had become friends with Saddam. But Yemen's real problem in 1990 was its seat on the UN Security Council. It normally could have remained neutral and stayed out of sight, but being on the Security Council it had to vote for or against the strict sanctions Bush and his allies were determined to impose on Iraq. Yemen either abstained or voted no, the only council member not to support the isolation of Iraq aside from Cuba. In his memoirs, Bush writes, "I knew Ali Abdallah Saleh and didn't feel he would recklessly side with Saddam" at first. But by November 1990 Yemen had abstained or voted no on all the key UN resolutions condemning Iraq and imposing sanctions. It voted no on the critical resolution, 678, authorizing the use of force to liberate Kuwait.[18]

The reaction was immediate and costly. In September 1990, the Saudis expelled over a million Yemeni guest workers in the kingdom who came home with no money and no jobs. Many ended up in wretched refugee camps. The Bush administration cut all economic assistance to Yemen in November. The newly united Republic of Yemen was now broke and abandoned by its traditional benefactors.

The Saudis went further and accused Saleh of being part of a conspiracy to divide the Arabian Peninsula. Iraq would take Kuwait, the Eastern Province of Saudi Arabia (home to its oil wealth), Bahrain, Qatar, and the UAE. Baghdad would control the world's energy. King Hussein of Jordan would get the Hejaz, where his great-grandfather had ruled until World War I. Saleh and Yemen would take back the Asir and Najran, the area lost to Saudi Arabia in the 1934 war between the two. There was no evidence of this tripartite conspiracy, but Riyadh pushed the claim relentlessly in its public statements. Saudi ambassador to the United States Prince Bandar bin Sultan was particularly active in publicizing the charge.

Bush did not believe in the conspiracy, but he was deeply disappointed in Saleh. Yemen's relations with America became toxic. He tried to persuade Saleh to join the coalition over the phone. Bush later recalled the call as "kind of pathetic."[19] When the crisis ended with the rapid liberation of Kuwait by the coalition's military, Yemen did not join the celebrations. It was an outcast. Unlike King Hussein, whom Bush needed to move forward the Arab-Israeli peace process, as he had promised the Arabs before the liberation, Yemen had nothing to offer. The new Republic of Yemen was alone.

In 1993 William Jefferson Clinton inherited Bush's policy toward Yemen. Other issues had much higher priority in the Middle East. Clinton faced hostile Iraq and Iran; he pursued a policy known as dual containment to keep them under some measure of control. He was much more interested in pursuing the Arab-Israeli peace process, especially after the Norwegians announced that they had facilitated direct negotiations between Israel and the Palestine Liberation Organization in Oslo.

CIVIL WAR, 1994

If America was fairly quick to forget about Yemen's role in the Kuwait crisis, Saudi Arabia was not, and it was eager for revenge against Saleh. Yemen was the responsibility of Saudi defense and aviation minister Prince Sultan bin Abd al-Aziz, the half brother of King Fahd. Sultan was also the father of the Saudi ambassador to the United States, Prince Bandar bin Sultan, whom I had worked closely with since the invasion of Kuwait in August 1990.

The Saudis looked to break up the Republic of Yemen and restore southern independence. They had numerous resources to work with. All the former sheikhs and sultans who had ruled the provinces of the south under the British had gone into exile in the Kingdom and were on pensions from the Saudis. They still had influence in their old homes and tribes. Many had returned home after unification in 1990 still on the Saudi payroll. The Saudis also recruited from the Communists who had merged with the north, who were increasingly disillusioned by Saleh's rule, in which they were sidelined by northerners.[20]

I returned to the Central Intelligence Agency in late 1993 to be national intelligence officer for the Near East and South Asia.

We began warning the White House that civil war was coming in Yemen soon and that the Saudis were behind southern secession. Vice President Beidh withdrew from Sana'a in August 1993, saying he could not work with Saleh. He presented publicly a long list of grievances by the south against the north. King Hussein of Jordan tried to mediate the two including a summit of the two hosted by Hussein in Amman in late February 1994. It was too late.

Fighting broke out on April 27, 1994; in a large tank battle near Sana'a, the southern forces were defeated by Saleh loyalists. The southern air force bombed Sana'a; the north did the same to Aden. The south fired Scud missiles at Sana'a. The south formally seceded on May 21, 1994, creating the Democratic Republic of Yemen, but the Saleh forces were already closing in on Aden.

The Saudis provided massive amounts of aid to the south, estimated at over $1 billion in aid and arms purchased from third parties, often former Soviet client states or newly freed parts of the former Soviet Union.[21] Prince Sultan and his son Bandar engineered many of the sales. In many cases the equipment arrived too late and was captured by the northern forces. As national intelligence officer, I followed closely the Saudi aid effort; it was massive but not well executed.

Saleh portrayed the southern rebellion as a Saudi plot to divide Yemen so that Saudi Arabia could seize the Hadhramaut and Mafrah provinces in the east and annex them to the Kingdom. An oil pipeline would follow. The Saudi hand alienated many Yemenis.

Bandar pressed the United States to help the rebels and recognize the Democratic Republic of Yemen. Clinton preferred to remain out of the battle, and the United States expressed support for the unity and territorial integrity of Yemen. It was a rare case of Washington not following Riyadh's bidding on Yemen. There was considerable concern in Washington that a southern state would be unstable, radical, and sympathetic to Saddam and Iraq.

Saleh got assistance from Islamic radicals in the north who wanted to destroy the remnants of communism in the south and impose their jihadist views on Aden. Some of these were Yemenis who had fought in Afghanistan. Southerners who had fled in 1986 during the south's brief civil war also came back, with Saleh now to regain power.

On July 4, 1994, Aden fell to Saleh's forces, and the rest of the south was regained quickly after that. The Republic of Yemen was restored. A general amnesty was proclaimed. Beidh went into exile in Oman.

Relations between the Clinton administration and the Saudis were strained. In a bid to restore them, I was sent to Riyadh, Khamis Mushayt, and other Saudi military facilities with a small team of experts to discuss why the south had lost. It seemed an odd mission at first, but the White House wanted it, and I began to see that it was a way to let Sultan save face with his brothers. It was not his fault the plot had failed; the blame lay with the southerners. The briefings, accompanied by lots of satellite imagery, were well received.

At the end of the trip, it was time to brief Prince Sultan in person. Bandar was there and extremely nervous about how it would go over with his father. Sultan listened closely as Bandar translated my brief. Toward the end I showed Sultan evidence that military equipment purchased by the Saudis was now in Saleh's possession. Sultan burst out laughing for reasons unknown, and the tension in the room evaporated. Bandar was very grateful, and Washington and Riyadh went on to other issues.

I also visited Yemen in April 1995. Naturally, the trip began in Sana'a with extensive meetings with the embassy staff and then a fascinating tour of the old city of the capital, an architectural gem. Then I and several embassy personnel flew to Aden. Yemeni Airways provided plastic bags for all the passengers so that qat chewers would spit the leaves into a receptacle instead of onto the floor. Everyone (except me) chewed on the flight. In Aden we stayed in what had formerly been the Cuban intelligence service's villa, now rented by the embassy. The chef was a former member of the Popular Front for the Liberation of Palestine.

We visited the famous crater in the center of the city where the National Liberation Front had fought the British in 1968, forcing their withdrawal and heralding the creation of the only Communist country in the Arab world. There was extraordinarily little mark of the Soviets' decades-long presence in the city. We did go swimming in the ocean, and I had the best lobster dinners I have ever had. Our rented jeep did get mired down once in the sand dunes; a Bedouin on a camel came by and showed us how to gain traction.

For the Clinton administration Yemen receded to its usual standing as a backwater. I moved on to a job at the Pentagon in 1995 and then back to the White House in 1997 as special assistant to the president and senior director for Near East and South Asia affairs at the National Security Council. For the next three years my attention was focused on the Arab-Israeli issue, Iraq, Iran, and South Asia.

YAFPAK

YEMEN AND THE WAR ON TERRORISM

The October 2000 attack on the USS *Cole*, an American destroyer, in Aden harbor dramatically changed America's relations with Yemen and set the foundation for the next decade of American policy toward the country. Ali Abdallah Saleh would become a frequent guest at the White House, but he never tackled the terrorist problem at home as effectively and single-mindedly as three presidents urged.

Bill Clinton hosted Saleh for a visit to the White House in April 2000. He had previously met the Yemeni president at the funeral for King Hussein in Amman on February 8, 1999. In 2000 Clinton had just returned from an extraordinarily successful visit to India, which included short stops in Bangladesh, Pakistan, and Oman, as well as a meeting with Syrian president Hafez Assad in Geneva, Switzerland. He was focusing his attention on trying to resolve the Arab-Israeli conflict. Saleh was in Washington from April 2 to 4. The threat of al-Qaeda was very much on the president's agenda. He and his national security adviser, Samuel "Sandy" Berger, regarded al-Qaeda as the number one threat to American national security. Clinton and Berger had already tried to kill Osama bin Laden once in his hideout in Afghanistan.

In fact, Saleh monopolized the meeting with a half-hour recitation of all the problems Yemen faced.[1] Clinton barely got a word in before it was time to move on to another visitor. Saleh promised all the right things; there was little follow-up.

The Clinton administration did promise to use Aden harbor more frequently for refueling US Navy ships. Normally this was done in Djibouti, where the French had a naval base. The bombings of the American embassies in Kenya and Tanzania in August 1998 had raised questions about the security of any city in East Africa.

Clinton was a remarkably busy president in October 2000. The failure of the Camp David talks between the Israelis and Palestinians had set the stage for the second Palestinian intifada, which was raging in the West Bank and Gaza by October. Clinton and Central Intelligence Agency (CIA) director George Tenet were trying without success to bring the violence to a halt. Clinton's wife, Hillary, was running for senator from New York.

On October 12 the US Navy destroyer *Cole* was attacked by a suicide team in the harbor at Aden. The *Cole* arrived in Aden around 8:30 that morning and tied up at a mooring to start taking on fuel. Two suicide bombers maneuvered their small boat up to the *Cole* and at 11:22 set off their explosives, blowing a forty-foot hole in the destroyer. Seventeen sailors died in the attack. HMS *Marlborough*, a British frigate, came to the rescue and helped to stabilize the *Cole*.

It was early morning in Washington. I got a call from the White House Situation Room and headed to work early. President Clinton was at his new family home in Chappaqua, New York, with Hillary and Chelsea. Suspicion immediately focused on al-Qaeda, but the intelligence community had no evidence to back up suspicions. As Clinton wrote later, "We all thought it was the work of bin Laden and al Qaeda, but we couldn't be sure." Clinton called President Saleh, who was in Aden and promised full cooperation to fight the terrorists and investigate the bombing.[2]

Teams of investigators went to Aden, overwhelming the embassy, to collect evidence. The lead Federal Bureau of Intelligence (FBI) investigator, Lebanese American Ali Soufan, had considerable expertise in such work. By the end of October, the FBI team had developed an "intelligence case" that al-Qaeda was responsible.[3] But back in Washington, CIA director George Tenet told the White House that the agency could not link bin Laden directly to the attack. Moreover, the CIA had no targets for a retaliatory strike beyond those already hit after the East Africa bombings.[4]

Saleh repeatedly blamed the bombing on the Israeli secret intelligence service, the Mossad.[5] Clinton and I went to Sharm el-Sheikh in Egypt to meet with Israeli prime minister Ehud Barack and Palestinian chairman Yasser Arafat, along with Egyptian president Husni Mubarak and Jordan's King Abdallah, to try to end the intifada and restore peace negotiations. The trip was a failure. On returning to Washington, Clinton went to Norfolk, Virginia, for a memorial service for the sailors lost on the *Cole*. Shortly afterward, the presidential election resulted in a hung outcome. Neither Vice President Al Gore nor George W. Bush was a clear winner. Decision making in Washington was also in limbo.

For the next decade, counterterrorism would be the top issue between America and Yemen; it dominated every other issue by far. President Saleh made four visits to Washington during the Bush administration, all of them focused on terrorism.

Al-Qaeda had deep roots in Yemen. Osama bin Laden's father was from the Hadhramaut in southern Yemen. Bin Laden had sought Saudi government approval to launch an insurgency in the south against the People's Democratic Republic of Yemen after he returned from Afghanistan in 1989; the Saudi princes turned him down, but he went ahead anyway and built up a cadre in the south. His deputy, Ayman Zawahiri, spent considerable time in

Yemen in the 1990s even though he was a wanted man in Egypt.[6] More than two thousand Yemenis joined al-Qaeda in Iraq after the American invasion.[7] Of the fifteen hijackers on September 11, nine came from parts of Saudi Arabia closely affiliated with Yemen.[8]

Saleh came to Washington just after 9/11 to see Bush in late November 2001. I was in the meeting. I warned Bush not to let Saleh filibuster the meeting as he had with Clinton. Bush was very straightforward and pressed Saleh to take clear and effective action against al-Qaeda in Yemen. He was given specific names of terrorists to be apprehended. Already the media were reporting that Bush was blaming Iraq for supporting bin Laden and planning to invade Iraq after Afghanistan. Saleh made an offer to mediate with Saddam to better relations between Baghdad and Washington. He quoted an Arab saying that you should not put a cat in cage because it could turn into a lion. Bush retorted that this cat had rabies and needed to be killed.[9]

Saleh also visited the Pentagon, where he saw firsthand the damage done by the terrorists. He was promised considerable new military equipment if he moved against al-Qaeda.[10] But on the ground in Yemen, little was done to fight al-Qaeda by Saleh's government. Yemen's counterterrorism agencies and security forces were infiltrated by Islamic extremists with ties to al-Qaeda and its allies.[11]

The problem was compounded by Yemen's incredible gun culture. In 2007 it was estimated that there were up to sixty million weapons in a nation of about twenty million citizens. These were not just small arms and the ubiquitous AK-47 assault rifle but also artillery, mortars, and heavy machine guns. Yemen is the second most heavily armed society in the world behind the United States, and it was and remains easy for terrorists and militia groups to be well armed. Saleh tried to limit the number of gun sellers in 2007 but had no impact.[12]

Saleh was back in Washington to see Bush in June 2004, November 2005, and May 2007. Each time he was pressed to do more, and many promises were made. Yemen remained a safe harbor for al-Qaeda. On September 17, 2008, the American embassy in Sana'a was attacked, and ten Yemenis were killed in the firefight between the terrorists and the security forces.

The American invasion of Iraq in 2003 was a big boost to al-Qaeda in Yemen. The war and subsequent occupation were very unpopular in Yemen, seen as nothing more than naked aggression and imperialism. Many Yemenis, including Saleh, had long-standing connections to Iraq and sympathized with the Iraqi people. Hundreds of Yemenis went to Iraq to join the insurgency.

Barack Obama campaigned in 2008 as an opponent of the decision to invade Iraq. I was on his campaign team, and in January 2009, he called me and asked that I chair an interagency study of our policy toward Afghanistan and Pakistan, or AFPAK, as the study was named. In late January al-Qaeda in the Arabian Peninsula announced that it was headquartered in Yemen. Briefly the White House considered adding Yemen to the study. It would have been called YAFPAK; fortunately, wiser heads prevailed.

John Brennan, Obama's homeland security adviser and a former senior intelligence liaison in Saudi Arabia, became the administration's Yemen expert and interlocuter. John, whom I have known since the late 1970s, made four trips to Yemen to see Saleh between 2009 and 2011. Aid to Yemen soared up to $150 million in 2009 and higher in 2010. The administration's concern about terrorism in Yemen escalated further when an al-Qaeda terrorist attempted to blow up an airliner flying from Amsterdam to Detroit as it descended on Christmas Day 2009. The bomb had been made in Yemen and would have exploded the plane if the bomber had successfully triggered it. It was a very close call. The district attorney for Michigan asked me to be an expert witness for the prosecution. There was no doubt this was an al-Qaeda plot: the bomber had already made his martyrdom video taking credit for the attack. He was labeled the "underwear bomber" by the media, but it was a very serious threat.

ARRIVAL OF THE HOUTHIS

Al-Qaeda in Iraq was not the only unintended beneficiary of the Bush decision to invade Iraq; it also radicalized the Houthi movement in Yemen. The Houthis are Zaydi Shiites, or *Zaydiyyah*. Shiite Muslims are the minority community in the Islamic world, and Zaydis are a minority of Shiites, significantly different in doctrine and beliefs from the Shiites who dominate in Iran, Iraq, and elsewhere (often called Twelvers for their belief in twelve imams).

The *Zaydiyyah* take their name from Zayd bin Ali, the great-grandson of Ali, Muhammad's cousin and son-in-law, whom all Shiites revere. Zayd bin Ali led an uprising in 740 against the Umayyad Empire, the first dynastic empire in Islamic history, which ruled from Damascus. Zayd was martyred in his revolt, and his head is believed to be buried in a shrine to him in Kerak, Jordan. Zaydis believe he was a pure caliph who should have ruled instead of the Umayyads.

The distinguishing feature of Zayd's remembered biography is that he fought against a corrupt regime. Sunnis and Shiites agree that he was a righteous man. The Zaydi elevate him as a symbol of the fight against corruption. The Houthis have made fighting corruption the centerpiece of their political program, at least nominally. The Zaydi do not believe in ayatollahs like the Twelver Shiites—the Shiite sect in Iran and most of the Muslim world—nor do they practice the other Twelver doctrine of *taqqiyah* (dissimulation), which permits one to disguise his or her faith for self-protection. In short, this sect is vastly different from the Iranian version of Shiism that Americans have come to know since the 1979 Iranian Revolution.

Followers of Zayd established themselves in North Yemen's rugged mountains in the ninth century. For the next thousand years, the Zaydis fought for control of Yemen with varying degrees of success. A succession of Zaydi imams ruled the community, and Zaydis were the majority of the population in the mountains of the north. They fought against both the Ottomans and the Wahhabis in the eighteenth and nineteenth centuries.

The Houthis emerged as a Zaydi resistance to Saleh and his corruption in the 1990s led by a charismatic leader named Hussein al-Houthi, from whom they are named. The Houthi family are Hashemites—that is, descendants of the Prophet Muhammad.[13] They charged Saleh with massive corruption to steal the wealth of the Arab world's poorest country for his own family, much like other Arab dictators in Tunisia, Egypt, and Syria. They also criticized Saudi and American backing for the dictator.

The American invasion of Iraq in 2003 deeply radicalized the Houthi movement, as it did many other Arabs. It was a pivotal moment. The Houthis adopted the slogan "God is great, death to the US, death to Israel, curse the Jews, and victory for Islam" in the wake of the US-led invasion of Iraq. The group also officially called itself Ansar Allah, or "supporters of God." It was a turning point largely unrecognized outside Yemen, another unanticipated consequence of George Bush's Iraq adventures.

Hezbollah, the Shiite movement in Lebanon, which successfully expelled the Israeli army from the country, became a role model and mentor for the Houthis. Although made up of different kinds of Shiites, the two groups have a natural attraction. Hezbollah provided inspiration and expertise for the Houthis. Iran was a secondary source of support, especially since the Houthis and Iranians share a common enemy in Saudi Arabia. Both began training Houthi fighters in Lebanon and Iran and sent advisers to Yemen to train them there.

After 2003, Saleh launched a series of military campaigns to destroy the Houthis. In 2004, Saleh's forces killed Hussein al-Houthi. The Yemeni army and air force were used to suppress the rebellion in the far north of Yemen, especially in Saada province. The fighting took place in fits, with occasional cease-fires.

Qatar tried to mediate a permanent end to the fighting, but it failed. The United States backed Saleh with military aid under the rubric of fighting terrorism. Washington devoted extraordinarily little attention to studying the Houthis and their base of support.

Shortly after Obama came into office, Saleh announced an all-out offensive against the Houthis in August 2009 called Operation Scorched Earth. The Yemeni air force attacked civilian targets using American-made jets. On November 4, 2009, the Houthis attacked a Saudi border installation and seized Saudi territory. They accused the Saudis of backing Saleh, which was true. The Saudis responded with heavy airstrikes on Saada, the stronghold of the Houthis.

The Houthis won against both Saleh and the Saudi army, besting them both again and again. For the Saudis, who have spent tens of billions of dollars on their military, it was deeply humiliating. In 2010 the Houthis asked Iraqi grand ayatollah Ali al-Sistani to mediate the dispute. The Saudis were outraged that an Iraqi Shia holy man would be shaping the future of their neighbor. The Saudis and Saleh announced Operation Blow to the Head in yet another effort to defeat the Houthis; it too failed.

There was a comical aspect to the deadly conflict. Saleh renamed Sana'a's Iran Street as Neda Agha Soltan Street after a young Iranian girl killed in protests against the Iranian regime in 2009. Tehran responded by renaming a major boulevard The Martyrs of Saada Street.[14]

THE ARAB SPRING

The Arab Spring came to Yemen in 2011. The Houthi movement joined the wide national uprising against Saleh. The movement was angry that Saleh's family was given lucrative jobs in the military and economy that benefited the family. His sons were in command of the Republican Guard and other elite formations in and around the capital. Other relatives ran the oil industry. The Saudis stood by Saleh at first but increasingly saw the need for a political solution. Significant elements of the army defected to the rebels, and a standoff ensued.

Saleh blamed Israel and the United States for the unrest, saying the protests were directed from Tel Aviv and the White House. Then he called to apologize to Brennan.[15] The Obama administration was concerned that if Saleh were removed by the protests, chaos would ensue in Yemen, opening the door further to al-Qaeda. So it urged calm and dialogue.

On June 3, 2011, Saleh was severely injured when a bomb went off in the mosque in the Presidential Palace in Sana'a. Seven of his bodyguards were killed. Saleh was flown to Saudi Arabia the next day for medical treatment. He was severely burned and had shrapnel wounds. Abdrabbuh Mansour Hadi, Saleh's vice president and a southerner, took command while Saleh recovered. Saleh returned to Yemen in September.

In November, under intense pressure from the Saudis, Saleh agreed to transfer power permanently to Hadi in exchange for immunity from prosecution. An election in February 2012 selected the only candidate on the ballot, Hadi, to take office. Saleh moved to Oman and then to the United States for further medical treatment.

A national dialogue was instituted to address the future of Yemen after Saleh, with regional and international assistance. It proposed a federal solution with six semiautonomous provinces. The Zaydi-dominated north got two landlocked entities, which the Houthis argued constituted gerrymandering against them.

In 2014, they began secretly colluding with Saleh against Hadi. Even by the standards of Middle Eastern politics, it was a remarkable and hypocritical reversal of alliances by both the Houthis and Saleh. Much of the army remained loyal to Saleh and his family, so together with the Houthis, the two had a pre-ponderance of force in the country. Hadi was deeply unpopular and increasingly seen as a Saudi stooge.

After months of gradual encroachment on the capital, Sana'a fell to the rebel alliance in January 2015, just as King Salman ascended to the throne in Riyadh. The Houthis opened direct civilian air traffic between Sana'a and Tehran, Iran promised cheap oil for Yemen, and rumors of more Iran-Houthi cooperation spread quickly.[16] The main port at Hudaydah fell to the Houthi forces, and they began marching to take Aden, the capital of the south and the largest port on the Indian Ocean.

Obama and the War's Origins

BARACK OBAMA'S TOP PRIORITY IN THE MIDDLE EAST WAS TO reach an agreement that would prevent Iran from getting a nuclear weapon. More broadly, he wanted to end the conflict between America and Iran that dated to 1979 and the hostage crisis. Yemen was far down his administration's priority list. Terrorism had dominated America's agenda with Yemen for a decade, and al-Qaeda was still lethal and dangerous; the Houthis were barely on Washington's screen. As a result, the Obama administration went with its default position and backed Saudi Arabia's disastrous decision to intervene in Yemen's civil war against the Houthis and Saleh. Obama's Iran policy was a brilliant success but came at a cost to Yemen. The resulting quagmire continues to this day. There was no serious consideration of alternatives in 2015 and 2016.

King Abdallah of Saudi Arabia died on January 23, 2015. He had been ill for some weeks. Abdallah had been the Kingdom's ruler for two decades, first as regent for his half brother Fahd, who had suffered a debilitating stroke in 1995, and then as king after Fahd died in 2005. Before then he had been in charge of the Saudi National Guard for almost a half century and understood better than most the strengths and weaknesses of the Saudi military. As crown prince in 1990, he had supported Fahd's decision to invite the United States to send a half million troops to defend the Kingdom in Operation Desert Shield and then liberate Kuwait in Operation Desert Storm.

Abdallah had been a cautious man not prone to impetuous decisions. He was also risk averse; he did not like taking chances unless they were essential. He preferred to rely on diplomacy over force, and if force was necessary, he preferred it to be supplied by Americans, not Saudis. He was open to dialogue with Iran despite the years of hostility between Riyadh and Tehran; he had even appointed a Shia as the Saudi ambassador to Iran. In 2014 and 2015 he was alarmed by the deteriorating situation in Yemen and the rise of the Houthis, but he did not want to send in Saudi troops. He remembered well that Egypt had done so in the 1960s and become bogged down in a quagmire that Saudi Arabia had fueled.

Abdallah's successor was Crown Prince Salman, a half brother and descendant of King Abdelaziz Al Saud, the founder of the modern Kingdom. Salman had outlived several brothers who had died while crown princes, including Sultan, commander of the Saudi military for fifty years, and Nayef, the minister of the interior for almost as long. Salman had been governor of Riyadh province for over a half century during which the Saudi capital grew from a small town of fewer than one hundred thousand people into a modern city of seven million with shopping malls, highways, and desalinated water piped in from the Persian Gulf. Because most the Saudi royal family lived in Riyadh, he was also the policeman of the family and knew all the secrets of its princes and princesses.

What Salman lacked was foreign policy experience. He had dealt with the foreign diplomatic corps in Riyadh, but on issues of security and living requirements, not policy decisions. In that sense he was not as well prepared as Abdallah or Sultan for the job of king. Sultan was, as we have seen, the preeminent expert on Yemen for decades; his voice was gone in 2015.

The king relied heavily on the opinions of one of his younger sons, Muhammad bin Salman (MBS), who had just turned thirty. MBS became minister of defense when his father ascended to the throne in January 2015. He had no experience in military matters, had never served in the military, and had no education in military science. He had been educated entirely in the Kingdom, with no overseas schooling. He did not speak English and wore a beard, unusual for a royal. He did not have any experience in traveling in the United States. He was impetuous and strong willed. He became the driver of Yemen policy for the new king.

Saudi royal decision making is not transparent. We simply don't know who supported going to war in 2015. The views of Crown Prince Muqrin, a former head of intelligence, are unknown. Prince Muhammad bin Nayef, the deputy crown prince, was concerned the war would divert attention and resources from fighting terrorism. The commander of the National Guard, the Kingdom's praetorian guard force, was not consulted at all and only learned about war after it started.[1] Foreign Minister Saud al-Faysal, a very experienced diplomat, was apparently against intervention, but his health was fading. It was very much Muhammad bin Salman's one-man show.

The decision to intervene was the result of a combination of panic about the Houthis' advances and their ties to Iran, with an unwarranted belief that defeating them would be easy and cheap. Obama's Saudi expert and Central Intelligence Agency (CIA) director, John Brennan, wrote later that he met with MBS just before the war began: "The prince said confidently, 'We'll finish off the Houthis in a couple of months, and then turn our attention to cleaning up the situation in the north,' an apparent reference to Syria and Iraq. I looked to him with a rather blank stare and wondered to myself what he had been smoking."[2] Other Saudi officials also told their American counterparts the war would be over in a few weeks.[3]

To support the Saudi intervention, Prince Salman and his father sought to organize a multinational coalition of states to send troops or air and naval support for what they called Operation Decisive Storm. Jordan, Bahrain, Qatar, and Morocco, for example, promised some air support. Egypt, with its memories of the 1960s, offered only some naval support, no troops on the ground or air support. Oman, Yemen's only other neighbor, did not join the coalition. Sultan Qaboos was too smart about wars in Yemen to join a loser.

The Saudis did get support from the United Nations. The United Nations Security Council passed a resolution on April 14, 2015, backing the Hadi government, endorsing the coalition's use of force, calling for an arms embargo on the Houthis alone, and demanding they give up their arms and surrender the territory they had acquired since 2014. Resolution 2216 also sanctioned Houthi leader Abdulmalik al-Houthi and Ahmed Ali Abdallah Saleh (Saleh's son) for their role in the rebellion against the Hadi government. Only the Russians spoke out against the resolution as unbalanced and unhelpful, but they abstained and did not veto it.

FAILURE WITH PAKISTAN

The war opened on March 25, 2015, with the Saudi-led coalition imposing a naval and air blockade on the Houthi-controlled north of Yemen. The main port of Hudaydah and Sana'a airport were closed. The Saudis and their partners began air attacks on Houthi and Saleh forces. Hadi fled first to Aden and then to Riyadh. Saudi ground forces, the regular army and the National Guard, had their hands full with protecting border posts and towns from the Houthis; there was no army to march on Sana'a.

Most critically, the Saudis wanted help from Pakistan. Pakistan had been an important Saudi ally for decades. In the early 1980s, after the Iranian Revolution removed the shah and the Soviets invaded Afghanistan, the Saudis had turned to Pakistan for protection. The then dictator of Pakistan, General Zia ul Huq, sent a reinforced brigade of Pakistani troops to the Kingdom to help defend it from foreign and domestic foes. Based in the northwest of the Kingdom at Tabuk, not far from Israel, the 12th Khalid bin Walid Independent Armored Brigade grew in size to muster twenty thousand men at its peak. The Saudis paid all the expenses. It was posted in the Kingdom from 1982 to 1986, and Pakistani advisors stayed on for decades afterward.[4]

In 2015 Muhammad bin Salman asked Pakistan to send a similar force to be the ground troops for a march on Sana'a, knowing the Saudis could not do it by themselves. Pakistani prime minister Nawaz Sharif was summoned to Riyadh to hear the prince's pitch. According to Sharif and his aides, however, who talked to me extensively about their conversations with the Saudis, the Saudi argument was weak and unconvincing. MBS had no strategy for winning the war and no end game for what to do with the Houthis and Saleh. To Sharif the Saudi plea looked like a prescription for bogging down a large division-size force in a hopeless quagmire in Yemen for years to come.

Pakistan has a large Shia minority sympathetic to its brothers in Yemen. It also shares a long border with Iran; thus it has no interest in being drawn into the sectarian rivalry between Tehran and Riyadh.

Saying no to Riyadh was not easy for Islamabad. To protect his domestic position, Sharif took the issue to the Pakistani parliament, which voted unanimously in favor of defending Saudi Arabia and against sending any troops to the Kingdom. So did the Pakistani army, which could see for itself that Yemen was a war it wanted no part of. So, the crucial element of MBS's plan was gone.[5]

American Response

Barack Obama was in India on a state visit when King Abdallah died. Obama had already visited the Kingdom on several occasions in his time in office; he courted Abdallah despite Saudi support for repression in the Arab Spring. Now he cut short the visit, cancelling a trip to the Taj Mahal with the First Lady to fly to Saudi Arabia to pay his respects to the royal family. Originally Vice President Joe Biden was supposed to attend the funeral, but Obama wanted to make clear his priority, keeping the Saudis in a strong alliance with Washington and his administration.[6] Ties had been strained during the Arab Spring when Obama flirted with support for the new regime in Egypt and even political change in Bahrain. He wanted them fully back on track as he pushed the Iran nuclear deal forward.

Yemen certainly was a topic of discussion for Obama with King Salman. It is unknown if the king asked for American support in fighting the Houthis, but he most certainly expressed concern about the rebels and their ties to Iran. Certainly, Obama did not put down a marker against a Saudi intervention in Yemen. The Americans were comfortable with Muhammad bin Nayef playing a large role in the king's party; he was trusted by the CIA and the White House.

Obama's priority was the Joint Comprehensive Plan of Action (JCPOA) with Iran. It was the "signature" policy of his second term.[7] The intricate agreement to freeze Iran's nuclear weapons program was the product of intense negotiations between Iran and the permanent members of the UN Security Council: America, Great Britain, France, Russia, and China, plus Germany and the European Union. The agreement was very controversial in the United States. Israel was adamantly against it, and Prime Minister Benjamin Netanyahu lobbied loudly against the JCPOA, including directly with the US Congress.

The agreement was announced on July 14, 2015, and went into action on January 16, 2016. The UN Security Council endorsed it unanimously in July 2015. It failed to win two non-binding resolutions in the US Senate and House, however, in

September 2015, with many Democrats joining the Republicans in voting against it.

In this tense atmosphere the Obama administration was eager to avoid another ally becoming a vocal opponent of the deal. The available evidence suggests there was little if any serious discussion of whether to support the Saudi intervention in Yemen. The best record of the decision-making process by two National Security Council staff members calls it a "painful story." The Saudis approached Washington in March 2015 with a request for assistance in a war they had already decided to wage. "All agree the decision ultimately came without much debate. . . . [A] deeply ambivalent president gave the green light," they recall. "While the US was seeking a landmark agreement with the kingdom's sworn enemy," a negative answer to the Saudi request "could have brought Saudi-US relations to a breaking point."[8]

The American ambassador in Riyadh recalls the Saudis were convinced the Houthis were Iranian pawns, fully controlled by Tehran. The American intelligence community had a much more nuanced view.[9] MBS was obsessed with Iran and blamed Oman for tolerating arms smuggling from Iran to the Houthis. The United States drifted along with the Saudis, Ambassador Joseph Westphal recalls, and there was never a discussion of whether or not to cut off or limit the provision of spare parts and other critical equipment to the Royal Saudi Air Force.[10]

Crown Prince Muhammad bin Nayef visited Washington with MBS for discussions with the administration in 2016. There were no words of caution given to the Saudis. King Salman visited later in the year to see Obama; the Saudis were lauded for their alliance with America. MBS had a long visit to the United States in 2017, where he was applauded from New York to Los Angeles for his supposed "reformist" views. The fact that he was the architect of mass malnutrition in Yemen was ignored by sycophantic commentators like Tom Friedman of the *New York Times*.

The Saudis took other steps against Iran. Iranian aid to the Houthis was marginal, probably constituting around $10 million a year and a few advisers from the Iranian Revolutionary Guard Corps. In January 2016 the Saudis executed several Saudi Shia for alleged acts of treason, which sparked violent demonstrations at the Saudi diplomatic facilities in Iran. King Salman broke relations with Iran and urged other states to follow; Bahrain and the Maldives did. Iranians were excluded from the pilgrimage to Mecca, the Hajj, because of the break in relations.

Meanwhile American arms sales to the Kingdom soared on Obama's watch to well over a $100 billion. The largest single deal was negotiated by Secretary of Defense Robert Gates in the first term of Obama's presidency and was worth close to $70 billion.

In short, it was business as usual with the Saudis. The Iran threat would be countered by the JCPOA. Secretary of State John Kerry initiated a dialogue with his Iranian counterpart to discuss regional issues, especially the stability of Iraq. For the first time since the American embassy was seized in November 1979, Washington was engaged in a direct and productive dialogue with Tehran. It was a big success for Obama.

The al-Qaeda threat was countered by robust counterterrorism operations from a variety of bases in the region. Most of the organization's key leaders were dead, and of course Osama bin Laden had been killed by a commando strike in Abbottabad, Pakistan, in 2011. The problems of war and hunger in a small country on the southwestern tip of the Arabian Peninsula, the poorest country in the Middle East, were not a significant priority for Washington.

Yet there was an alternative to the course of backing the Saudis unconditionally. Washington could have assured Riyadh that the United States would help defend the Kingdom against any threats from Yemen. As had been the case with the JCPOA, a UN Security Council resolution would provide international endorsement for the Kingdom's defense. At the same time Washington could engage the Houthi leadership and former president Ali Abdallah Saleh and seek common ground for a political resolution of the Yemeni civil war. That solution might be based on accepting the Houthi-Saleh government in Sana'a while offering Aden and the south autonomy or even independence. This course of action would have nicely complemented Obama's Iran dialogue by opening a door to American relations with a pro-Iran Houthi-dominated North Yemen.

AFTER THE FACT

What is remarkable in the recollections after office of how the United States drifted into backing the Saudi war is how little the Obama team members recall the process in their memoirs. The war just doesn't register in these otherwise very complete histories of the Obama administration. Samantha Power, for example, was the American ambassador to the United Nations who secured the one-sided resolution from the Security Council that endorsed the Saudi war and called on the Houthis to give up their arms and surrender. There is not a single reference in her memoir to the war in Yemen or her role in getting the resolution passed. She does comment once on Yemen's view on gays.[11]

Susan Rice, Obama's national security advisor, does make a cryptic comment on the war in assessing the administration's record. "We remained reluctant to exert maximum pressure on our partners to take the steps they resisted—whether on the Saudis to end the war in Yemen or the Israelis and Palestinians to negotiate in good faith," she writes in her only substantive comment on the war.[12]

Secretary of State John Kerry, who negotiated the JCPOA and met often with his Iranian counterpart, has one mention of Yemen in his memoir: Iran was "meddling in Yemen." So he just repeats the Saudi argument without any comment in a book otherwise full of explanations for Iranian behavior.[13] His undersecretary for political affairs, Wendy Sherman, who did much of the secret diplomacy that led to the JCPOA, has nothing to say about Yemen.[14]

The collective amnesia suggests a profound sense of remorse. The Obama team knows it failed to act creatively in Yemen in 2015 and 2016.

CHAPTER 5

Trump and a Humanitarian Disaster

DONALD TRUMP FOLLOWED BARACK OBAMA IN OFFICE IN JANU-
ary 2017. He had lost the popular vote to Hillary Clinton but won
a narrow victory in the Electoral College. Trump had no previous
experience in government at any level. He had little experience
in foreign policy. He had achieved prominence as the leader of
the so-called birther movement, which denied Obama was a
legitimate president because he was allegedly born abroad, not
in Hawaii. Obama produced his birth certificate to prove he was
a legitimate citizen. The affair was an obvious effort to appeal to
white racists who hated having a black man in the White House
as the president of the United States.

The Yemen war was not an issue in the election. Instead,
Trump attacked the nuclear deal with Iran as the "worst deal
ever" and promised to withdraw America from the Joint Comprehensive Plan of Action if elected. It was part of a much broader
attack on many of the foundations of American foreign policy
in the last half century. Trump called the North Atlantic Treaty
Organization (NATO), the most successful alliance in the history of American alliances, "obsolete" and refused to endorse the
principle of collective defense. He rejected the NATO mission
in Afghanistan. He seemed closer to Russian dictator Vladimir
Putin than to any of America's traditional allies.

Trump was also very anti-Muslim. In the campaign he advo-cated a "total and complete shutdown of Muslims entering the United States." A "Muslim ban" became part of his platform. He also attacked Saudi Arabia, claiming it was responsible for the 9/11 attacks.[1] So it is deeply ironic that a man who was elected to ban Muslims from America so quickly became the chief advocate of the most puritanical country in the Islamic world.

Iran was the driver. Iran was the centerpiece of much of his foreign policy. Iran was held responsible for most of the unrest in the Middle East. Trump would embark on a policy of "max-imum pressure" on Iran using sanctions and targeted military operations against the Islamic Republic. All of this was received well in Riyadh, where King Salman's team was running the most intensely sectarian and anti-Iranian policy of any Saudi monarch. It was also well received in Israel.

TRUMP VISITS RIYADH

The first senior Trump administration official to visit the King-dom was his new director of central intelligence (DCI), Michael Pompeo. Pompeo previously had been a congressman from Kansas who had served on the House Intelligence Committee, which is how I met him. His trip to Riyadh was primarily to reinforce the already strong intelligence liaison relationship with the Saudis, especially the new crown prince, Muhammad bin Nayef. Nayef was well known to the Americans; he had led the fight from 2003 to 2006 against al-Qaeda in the Kingdom, which ended in the defeat of the terrorists. He also provided intelligence directly to John Brennan that prevented several terrorist attacks on American soil, including one in which al-Qaeda planned to put bombs on delivery aircraft flying from Europe to the United States, which would explode as they descended to land.

The trip was Pompeo's first overseas mission as DCI, an indi-cation of how important Saudi Arabia was for the new team. He consulted with me privately before the trip. Pompeo gave Nayef the George Tenet memorial counterterrorism medal, an honor created exclusively for the prince. He also began a discussion about a presidential visit to the Kingdom.

Defense Minister Muhammad bin Salman (MBS) then traveled to Washington to finalize plans for the president. MBS had already forged a friendship with Trump's son-in-law, Jared Kushner, behind the scenes. Kushner arranged the defense minister's appointments in Washington. He had a lucky break as well. A snowstorm in March 2017 prevented German chancellor Angela Merkel from landing in Washington; her lunch date with the president was given to MBS, so he got a sit-down meeting in the Oval Office, followed by lunch in the State Dining Room with the president as well.[2]

On May 20, 2017, President Trump arrived in Riyadh. The king met him at the airport, an unusual act for a Saudi monarch. It was Trump's first foreign trip in his administration; he was not even six months in office. No president had ever made Saudi Arabia his first foreign port of call. The visit coincided with several regional summits that King Salman was chairing. One was a meeting of the Gulf Cooperation Council, the collection of six monarchies on the Arab side of the Persian Gulf created for collective defense during the Iran-Iraq War. A second was a meeting of forty heads of state from across the Islamic world convened by the king in his role as protector of the holy cities. Included in the larger summit was the president of Egypt, the prime minister of Pakistan, and the king of Jordan, as well as all the Gulf monarchs except Sultan Qaboos of Oman.

The Saudis put on a major display of support for Trump, calculating correctly that he was very fond of flattery. The sides of skyscrapers in the capital bore his portrait. The summitry and posters covered up a serious lack of substance in the discussions. Although the administration claimed that the Saudis agreed to $110 billion in arms sales during the visit, in fact there were no new arms sales.

But there was agreement that Iran was the root of all evil in the region and must be confronted everywhere it operated. It was a "malign influence" and danger. Trump singled out the Iranians for offering terrorists "safe harbor, financial backing and the social standing needed for recruitment." They were responsible for "so much instability in the region."[3] That included Yemen. Trump endorsed enthusiastically the Saudi war in Yemen and fully agreed that the Houthis were pawns of the Iranians, who intended on setting up an Iran-aligned puppet state in the strategic southwest of the Arabian Peninsula, which could threaten the critical choke point between Africa and Asia.

So the summit put Yemen on the administration's list of priorities to support the Kingdom. But it offered no new means for the stalemate in the war to be broken. Indeed, the Houthis were getting stronger, and their missile capabilities were improving. The Saudis were stuck in a quagmire, one that had a terrible impact on the lives of millions of Yemenis.

Trump traveled from Riyadh to Jerusalem to see Bibi Netanyahu and the Israelis. They, of course, fully agreed that Iran was an evil and malign player intent on acquiring nuclear weapons that would pose an existential threat to Israel.

The trip illustrated dramatically Trump's priorities in the Middle East: supporting Saudi Arabia and Israel and confronting Iran. Yemen was collateral damage. Just a few weeks later King Salman fired Muhammad bin Nayef and replaced him as crown prince with his favorite son, Muhammad bin Salman. Nayef's lack of enthusiasm for the war in Yemen was a factor in his dismissal. MBS, the architect of a disastrous war, was now poised to be the next king of Saudi Arabia with the full approval of Donald Trump.

The *New York Times* ran an editorial stating that the "young and brash" prince was not ready for the job and that the Yemen war was proof that the "prince acts without thinking through the consequences of his decisions."[4]

The Stalemate Becomes a Quagmire

American military and intelligence support did not bring victory to the Saudis. Indeed, the war went from being a stalemate to a quagmire that cost the Kingdom billions of dollars. By the middle of 2017 the Houthis and their ally, Ali Abdallah Saleh, controlled virtually all of northern Yemen with the exception of Marib province in the east. The Houthis were the dominant player and imposed a brutal police state on the citizens of the north. But they had popular support as the defenders of Yemeni nationalism against the hated Saudis. They also played to their role as Zaydi Shia fighting Wahhabi Sunnis.

The Hadi government was only nominally in charge of the rest of Yemen. In Aden and the surrounding areas, real power was in the hands of southern separatists who longed to return to an independent South Yemen. Hadi himself spent most of his time in Riyadh. In the east along the Omani border, the Saudis were gradually taking direct control of the province of Al Mahra, giving them direct land access to the Indian Ocean from the Kingdom.

The blockade created an intensifying humanitarian catastrophe throughout Yemen, but especially in the north. Yemen imports much of its food and almost all of its medicine. With the Sana'a airport closed and the Hudaydah port shut, the population was literally being starved to death by the Saudis. The malnutrition of Yemeni children put them at higher risk of diseases that normally would be kept in check by healthy diets and appropriate medicine.

Trump and his team fully supported the blockade. They convinced themselves that it would eventually force the Houthis to surrender or at least halt the shipment of expertise and equipment from Iran to the Houthis. At a small cost to itself, compared to the huge cost of the Saudi war effort, Iran helped the Houthis develop more sophisticated missiles and drones, which they used to strike Saudi military bases near the border and, increasingly, Saudi cities as far away as Riyadh and Jidda.

As the year progressed the Saudis looked for a rupture in the Houthi-Saleh alliance to deliver them a victory. The Emiratis were particularly active in courting Saleh to break with the rebels and rejoin the Hadi team. It became an open secret that Saleh was flirting with Abu Dhabi. Of course, the alliance with the Houthis had always been a tactical maneuver. The two parties detested each other. Only a couple of years previously, the Houthis described Saleh as a "tyrant who only wants to please America and Israel."[5]

The crisis inside the rebel camp came to a head at the end of 2017. Armed clashes between the two factions began in late November. Saleh declared the split publicly on December 2, 2017. But there was no plan for how the Saudis and their allies would assist Saleh. In keeping with the general incompetence of MBS's war plans, there was no contingency plan to get aid to the former president if he actually broke with the Houthis. Emirati Crown Prince Mohammad bin Zayed, a close friend of MBS, was particularly inept in his planning.

On December 4, 2017, the Houthis attacked Saleh's home in Sana'a. He fled for Marib but was killed by a sniper's shot to the head in an ambush by the Houthis later that day. At seventy-five the man who famously danced on the heads of snakes was dead after ruling Yemen longer than anyone else in its modern history. The Houthis proclaimed that "the leader of the traitors" was gone. The Saudis and Emiratis had been proven again to be incompetent plotters.[6]

KHASHOGGI AND YEMEN

Millions of Yemenis had suffered for three years, but it was the death of one Saudi journalist in 2018 that finally soured the world and most Americans on Muhammad bin Salman. Jamal Khashoggi started his career working for the chief of Saudi intelligence, Turki al-Faysal, during the war against the Soviets in Afghanistan. He was a loyal supporter of the monarchy. But he was an early critic of the inept and dangerous crown prince.

He moved to America and began writing opinion pieces for the *Washington Post*. He wrote immediately after Saleh's death, "With Ali Abdallah Saleh's death Saudi Arabia is paying the price for betraying the Arab Spring." He decried the "secret deal between Saleh and Riyadh" that had failed so completely.[7]

In September 2018 he wrote an even more devastating critique of the prince's war in Yemen. Khashoggi noted that the war had "soured the Kingdom's relations with the world and harmed its reputation." He called on the prince to announce an immediate unilateral cease-fire and offer direct negotiations with the Houthis in Taif, Saudi Arabia. He correctly said the war was costing Saudi Arabia a fortune, while it cost Iran and the Houthis a pittance. For example, the Houthis' missiles and drones were manufactured in tiny factories in Yemen from spare parts from old cars and other appliances, while the Patriots the Saudis used to shoot them down cost $3 million apiece.

Khashoggi compared MBS to Syrian dictator Bashar Assad, who was responsible for the deaths of tens of thousands of Syrians in the civil war that kept him in power. "The Crown Prince must bring an end to the violence and restore the dignity of the birthplace of Islam," he wrote.[8]

It was his last piece. On October 2, 2018, Khashoggi entered the Saudi consulate in Istanbul, Turkey, to get some documents to prepare for his upcoming marriage. Inside was a special team of Saudi agents drawn from the crown prince's bodyguards and other elite formations; they murdered him in the consulate, mutilated his body, and destroyed parts of it. The assassins then fled back to the Kingdom in two private jets contracted by the crown prince's office.

Secretary of State Mike Pompeo called me the next day and told me that the worst was true: the crown prince had directly ordered the assassination. He asked my advice on what to do next. He ignored my suggestion to demand an immediate end to the blockade of Yemen and to cut off spare parts and expertise to the

Saudis until they adopted a complete cease-fire—in effect to use the human rights atrocity of one man as a pivot to end the much larger humanitarian catastrophe in Yemen. Instead, the Trump administration stood by Muhammad bin Salman. Trump even said he did not care if the crown prince was responsible.

The rest of America was appalled by the brutal murder of a journalist doing his job. Many of those who had hailed the crown prince during his tour of America now recanted. The US Congress passed resolutions denouncing the crime. But Trump stayed with the Saudis. He had already violated the nuclear deal with Iran in May 2018 and was wholly committed to the policy of confronting Iran and, by extension, the Houthis. The war became the worst humanitarian catastrophe in the world.

Opposition to the war began to rise in the United States. The combination of the Khashoggi murder and the horrendous humanitarian situation in Yemen sparked calls for a change in American policy. On the Hill there were efforts to limit or even cancel arms sales to the Kingdom and its partners in the Yemen war.

The Khashoggi murder also had a direct impact on US policy in Yemen. In the fall of 2018, the UAE created a task force of militiamen to seize the port of Hudaydah from the Houthis, their main seaport. After Khashoggi's death, Secretary of Defense James Mattis intervened with the Emiratis and Saudis to halt their offensive on the port, fearing it would create a bloody battle that would only encourage more legislative limits on US support for the coalition. Mattis's intervention led to the Stockholm Agreement in December 2018 in which the Emiratis agreed to pull back their attack force and the Houthis agreed to let observers oversee a cease-fire in the region around the port. The United Nations reported that the Houthis implemented the deal. UN Security Council Resolution 2019 created the United Nations Mission to Support the Hudaydah Agreement to oversee the cease-fire in the area. Subsequently the UAE withdrew its forces in North Yemen and concentrated all its activity in the south.

Air-to-air refueling of coalition warplanes en route to striking Yemen was halted, a small but significant step that particularly impacted the UAE because of the distance from Abu Dhabi to Yemen. The opposition was particularly strong among Democrats; in the Senate Christopher Murphy from Connecticut and Bernie Sanders from Vermont were outspoken opponents of America's role in the war. Hearings were held to galvanize votes. A few Republicans joined the opposition. But the votes were not there to change the overall approach of the Trump team. A new president would be needed to end America's role in the conflict.

In January 2020 Trump ordered the assassination of General Qassim Soleimani, the head of the Quds Force in the Iranian Revolutionary Guard who oversaw all of its operations worldwide. Soleimani was particularly focused on Iraq, Syria, and Lebanon, but he also worked with the Houthis in Yemen. He was killed arriving at Baghdad airport. The Houthis denounced the attack.

COVID AND YEMEN

In March 2020 a deadly virus, Covid, emerged from China to infect the world. The ensuing pandemic was a global disaster of unprecedented proportions. It would hit Yemen particularly hard because five years of war had already devastated the population. Even in the best of times, Yemen has little medical capability. Among the poor, medicine was often unavailable. Children were the most vulnerable.

By early 2020, 80 percent of the population, or twenty-four million people, required vast humanitarian assistance. Half were on the brink of starvation. Around two million children under five years old suffered from acute malnutrition. The war had devastated Yemen's primitive health care infrastructure; half of the country's medical facilities were dysfunctional. Doctors were scarce. Cholera was rampant throughout the country.[9]

To this situation the pandemic added further misery and death. Prior to the pandemic, two million children were out of school; the virus added another five million. The United Nations High Commission for Refugees said that the country's health care system had "in effect collapsed."[10] With the entire world reeling from the virus, raising funds to support humanitarian work in Yemen was increasingly difficult.

In the last days of his administration, Trump listed the Houthis as a foreign terrorist organization (FTO), a legal determination that severely limited any American or foreign organization from working with it for any purpose. The FTO determination was intended to tie the hands of any administration that sought to get help to the Yemeni people. It was a vindictive move.

Trump failed to deal with the virus at home. Hundreds of thousands of Americans died who would have lived with a competent leader running the country. The failure of the Trump administration to seriously address the disaster was key to the victory of Joseph Biden in November 2020. Biden immediately removed the FTO determination to allow the Yemeni people to get help.

CHAPTER 6

Biden and the Future

JOE BIDEN CAME TO THE PRESIDENCY WITH A WEALTH OF FOR-eign policy experience. For more than three and a half decades, he had been a senator, for much of that time serving on the Foreign Relations Committee. For eight years he was vice president to Barack Obama. His specific responsibility in the foreign affairs field was Iraq; the two had campaigned against the war in that country in 2008. Biden has his critics. Robert Gates, former secretary of defense and probably the most experienced intelligence and defense practitioner of his generation, said, "I think Biden has been wrong on nearly every major foreign policy and national security issue over the past four decades."[1] Gates was secretary when Biden led the withdrawal from Iraq, which led to the rise of the Islamic State terrorist organization.

Biden campaigned in 2020 on a plank of opposition to the Saudi war in Yemen; he was appalled by the murder of Jamal Khashoggi and promised to treat the Kingdom as a "pariah" for its human rights abuses. He did not stick with keeping it a pariah and visited the Kingdom in July 2022. He did promise to end the war in a speech in March 2021. A year later the United Nations announced a cease-fire between the warring parties to begin at the start of the Islamic holy month of Ramadan in April 2022. Biden's team deserves some of the credit for the truce, which partially lifts the Saudi blockade of Yemen and may relieve the humanitarian catastrophe seven years of war have brought. The United States essentially abandoned much of its flawed policy of those seven years, but it did so implicitly and behind the scenes. The cease-fire is fragile; it will need careful nurturing.

The United States needs to change further its policy toward Yemen and Saudi Arabia to end this catastrophic war. Ending the conflict is in the interest of Yemenis and the Kingdom of Saudi Arabia. It would also significantly reduce Iran's ability to project its influence into the Arabian Peninsula and bog down its rival in an expensive quagmire.

In the foreign policy debate among the Democrats seeking the nomination in 2019, Biden took center stage with a dramatic promise. He said, "I would make it very clear we were not going to sell more weapons" to the Saudis. He said that there was "very little social redeeming value in the present government in Saudi Arabia." Turning specifically to the Yemen war, Biden promised he would "end the sale of material to the Saudis where they are going in and murdering children." One of his key opponents, Senator Bernie Sanders, called the Kingdom a "brutal dictator-ship and not a reliable ally." None of the Democrats running for president supported Donald Trump's policy of total unconditional support for the Saudis and their war.

After his election Biden made clear that he personally would not deal with Crown Prince Muhammad bin Salman. He would not call him on the phone or meet with him. But his administra-tion would engage the crown prince.[2] As noted earlier, he lifted the designation of the Houthis as a foreign terrorist organization to allow aid to flow to the Houthi-controlled areas of Yemen.

Shortly after his inauguration Biden gave a major foreign policy speech. "The war in Yemen must end," he said as he named a new envoy for Yemen. Tim Lenderking is an experienced dip-lomat and Middle East specialist in the State Department. "He has worked on this file for years and is known to everyone who matters," wrote one expert. More specifically Biden promised an end to American support for "offensive" military operations by the Saudis, but he did not define what an offensive military action was or whether his admonition applied to the Saudi blockade of Yemen.[3]

Nor did Biden call for a new United Nations Security Council resolution (UNSCR) to serve as the basis for his peace initiative. As noted, UNSCR 2216 had called on the Houthis to withdraw from all territories they occupied in the civil war, including Sana'a, to recognize the Hadi government, to turn over their weapons to the United Nations, and to end missile attacks on Saudi Arabia. "After six years of fighting, not even one of these demands has been met by the Houthis," and the country is divided, with the Houthis controlling most of the population.[4] Biden did not mention that the resolution was deliberately tilted against the Houthis.

Much like his two predecessors, Biden was understandably focused more on Iran than on any other regional issue. He sought to undo Trump's decision to violate the Joint Comprehensive Plan of Action (JCPOA) on Iran's nuclear program. A special envoy, Robert Malley, was appointed to deal with reviving the JCPOA; he had written the most insightful article on Obama's Yemen policy by an insider a few years earlier. Progress on the Iran negotiations was slow at best, particularly after a new election brought to power hard-liners in the Iranian government.

Iran increased its profile in the Yemen war on Biden's watch. Tehran appointed Hassan Irlo to be its ambassador in Sana'a, the first ambassador accredited to the Houthi government. Irlo was a veteran of the Iran-Iraq War and a career official in the Iranian Revolutionary Guard. He was seriously wounded in the Iran-Iraq War by chemical weapons. He died in late 2021 from Covid and was buried back in Iran. Iran charged that the Saudis delayed allowing an evacuation flight from Sana'a that might have saved his life.[5]

The US Navy also continued to intercept vessels, usually small dhows, which it claimed were smuggling arms from Iran to the rebels. In December 2021, for example, the navy reported it had intercepted a vessel with 1,400 AK-47 assault rifles and 226,600 rounds of ammunition. In effect the United States was a partner in the Saudi blockade of Yemen.[6]

In August 2021 Biden withdrew American and North Atlantic Treaty Organization (NATO) forces from Afghanistan. He had promised an orderly withdrawal and a negotiated follow-on government. The whole operation was implemented incompetently. The withdrawal was a chaotic mess that turned into a complete victory for the Taliban. Two decades of American and NATO effort in Afghanistan collapsed in a month. It was a serious blow to the president's foreign policy, and his approval poll numbers at home took a very big hit; he went from being popular to unpopular with most Americans. Above all, his promise of delivering a competent foreign policy after the chaos of the Trump years was gone. The debacle cast a shadow over the rest of American foreign policy and raised doubts among allies about America's commitment to their defense.

Then, in March 2022, Russia invaded Ukraine. The Biden team had been warning for several months that such a blatant act of aggression was coming. It moved swiftly and effectively to rally the NATO alliance to support Ukraine with arms and diplomacy. The administration looked competent and in charge. The president visited Poland, the frontline state supporting Ukraine, and promised firm support for Ukraine and an ironclad commitment to use force to defend NATO members.

THE WAR IN YEMEN IN 2021

In 2021, despite Biden's promises, the war went on much as it had the previous five years. Saudi airstrikes continued across the country, and the blockade of Houthi-controlled areas continued unabated. Both are offensive operations that are supported by

American spare parts, technicians, intelligence, and other means. Less than 10 percent of the fuel needed to operate the Yemeni economy is being delivered to the country because of the blockade. Food and medicine are not getting to the people.

The costs of the war are staggering. One estimate is that Saudi Arabia has spent more than $100 billion on the war since 2015 and conducted more that twenty-three thousand airstrikes.[7] The cost to Yemenis of the war is horrific, perhaps bordering on genocide. The United Nations Development Programme estimated in November 2021 that 377,000 Yemenis have died in the war, most indirectly and not in combat. Seventy percent of these were children under the age of five, killed by malnutrition or disease. The UN report said almost five million Yemenis are malnourished. The Saudi blockade of Yemen is a principal cause of the humanitarian catastrophe in its denial of food and medicine to the country.[8]

American arms sales to Saudi Arabia have continued as usual, again despite Biden's campaign promises. A major deal to support the Saudi Apache attack helicopter fleet was signed in 2021 for a half million dollars. The Apache is an attack helicopter and has been widely used in the war to support offensive military operations. It is demonstrably not a defensive weapon.[9] A $650 million deal to sell air-to-air missiles was passed early in 2022. Senior US officials like National Security Advisor Jake Sullivan and climate czar John Kerry meet regularly with Crown Prince Muhammad bin Salman. French president Emmanuel Macron was the first Western head of state to meet with the prince in December 2021. He dismissed the murder of Jamal Khashoggi and said it should not be a barrier to working with the Saudis.

The al-Qaeda threat has significantly diminished in the last few years. Robust counterterrorism efforts by American and allied forces have been very successful in decapitating the organization and reducing its scope of operations. The last attack linked to al-Qaeda in the Arabian Peninsula (AQAP) occurred in 2019 and featured a Saudi soldier training in Pensacola, Florida, who turned out to be inspired by AQAP and killed several Americans before being killed by US forces.

The crucial battle of the war is now being fought in Marib, the only province in the north still largely in the hands of Hadi loyalists. Marib is east of Sana'a. It is home to the country's oil refinery. The country's oil pipeline runs from Marib to the coast. It is now full of refugees from other parts of the country who have sought safety in Marib. If it falls to Houthis, their conquest of North Yemen will be complete.

Meanwhile, the Saudis have focused their attention on the eastern governorate or province of Al Mahra, Yemen's second largest, which borders on Oman. Al Mahra is far from the Houthi-controlled territory in North Yemen and is populated by Sunni Muslims. Many of Al Mahra's residents are Mahri speakers, which further distinguishes them from the Arabic speakers throughout the rest of Yemen. It may have as many as three hundred thousand residents, although population estimates in Yemen are very speculative. Mahra has long been closely associated with the Omani province of Dhofar next door, which also has a small population of Mahri speakers.

Beginning in 2017, the Saudis gradually took control of Al Mahra.[10] They occupied the capital and the port and took control of the border posts with Oman. Saudi troops now control the province. Human Rights Watch reported that the Saudis and local allied tribes have used force, torture, and arbitrary detention to squelch any opposition to their occupation. The Saudis have twenty bases and outposts in the province now.[11]

Taking Al Mahra gives Saudi Arabia direct access to the Indian Ocean. Riyadh plans to build an oil pipeline from its Eastern Province through Al Mahra to the sea, according to some reports. That would ease Saudi dependence on the Strait of Hormuz for exporting oil, reducing the Iranians' potential leverage over Riyadh.

The Omanis are closely monitoring the Saudis' role in Al Mahra. Al Mahra was the base for Communist South Yemen to support the Dhofar rebellion in the 1970s, which was defeated after the shah of Iran sent troops to help the Omani army. Oman is the only Gulf monarchy that did not join the Saudi war coalition and has remained neutral in Yemen, often hosting foreign talks with the Houthis in Muscat. Sultan Qaboos decided in 2016 that the Saudi decision to intervene in Yemen was reckless and misguided. His successor is rightly concerned about the future of Yemen, especially the southeastern provinces of Al Mahra and Hadhramaut.

Abu Dhabi, on the other hand, is focused on Yemen's strategic islands. The UAE has downsized its role in the war in the last several years. The Emiratis have quietly chosen to get out of the Yemeni quagmire as much as possible and have substantially reduced their presence in Aden. They still have some small pockets of troops in Mokha, Shabwa, and a couple of other locations.

But they are very active on several key islands. Most recently, satellite imagery has shown that the UAE is building a major airbase on the island of Mayun, which is located in the Bab al-Mandab, or "Gate of Tears," the strait that links the Red Sea to the Gulf of Aden. Five square miles in size, the island is key to the control of the Bab al-Mandab.[12]

Mayun, also known as Perim, has been a goal of empires since ancient times. Portugal and the Ottoman Empire fought over it in the 1600s. The British grabbed it from the Ottomans in 1857 as the Suez Canal was built. The Communist People's Democratic Republic of Yemen (PDRY) took control in 1968 and together with Egypt blockaded the strait to Israel during the 1973 war. The Houthis took it in 2015, only to lose it to the Emiratis in 2016.

Abu Dhabi is also in control of the island of Socotra in the Gulf of Aden. Much larger than Mayun, Socotra has sixty thousand residents and is the largest island in the archipelago also named Socotra. Historically it was part of the sultanate of Mahra before becoming part of the PDRY. The Emiratis have a military base, which is used to collect intelligence on maritime traffic in the Bab al-Mandab and the Gulf of Aden. In 2022 there were press reports of Israeli tourists visiting Socotra as part of the Abraham Accords between Israel and the UAE. Thousands of Israelis have visited Dubai and Abu Dhabi, and apparently some are taking advantage of weekly flights to the island. The government of Yemeni president Abed Rabbo Mansour Hadi has protested the tourism and demanded Yemeni sovereignty be restored on the island, but Abu Dhabi long ago dismissed Hadi as ineffectual.[13]

The Houthis also denounced the Emiratis' activities in Socotra and Mayun, which they allege will create spy bases for both the UAE and Israel in these strategic waters.[14] Consequently, in January 2022 the Houthis began missile and drone attacks on Abu Dhabi.

Both Riyadh and Abu Dhabi are eager to get some advantage out of the expensive quagmire they jumped into in 2015. Territorial acquisition of strategic terrain may be the only gain possible. The acquisition may be de facto and never accepted by any Yemeni government. The fiction of Yemen's territorial integrity and sovereignty may cover the facts on the ground.

The United States should not be a party to the dismemberment of Yemen. It is not too early to quietly put down a marker that if a cease-fire is arranged in Yemen, the Saudis and Emiratis will need to evacuate Al Mahra, Mayun, and Socotra and return control to the Yemenis.

THE CEASE-FIRE

The cease-fire was arranged by the United Nations special envoy for Yemen, a Swedish diplomat named Hans Grunberg. Announced at the beginning of April 2022 for a two-month duration, the agreement halted all combat operations by both sides, including bombing by the Saudi air force and missile and drone attacks by the Houthis on Saudi Arabia and Abu Dhabi.

The agreement also opened Hudaydah to traffic, especially ships bearing fuel to restart Yemeni cities. It also mandated that Sana'a airport would be reopened to commercial flights to Amman, Jordan, and Cairo, Egypt.

The Saudis have also ditched Hadi, that man they installed in power a decade ago to replace Ali Abdallah Saleh. He is now under house arrest in Riyadh. He was replaced by a seven-man political council that represents the various groups still loyal to the Kingdom.

Quietly, behind the scenes, the Biden administration dumped seven years of American policy toward the war. The demands of UNSCR 1221 have been ignored. The Houthis are not going to evacuate Sana'a and other northern cities or unilaterally disarm. Washington has ceased asking for these unrealistic objectives; Riyadh has gone along. After seven years and billions of dollars, sense has prevailed.

The Houthis remain a dangerous and troubling party. Their intense anti-American and anti-Israeli rhetoric has not ceased. They have blamed Ukraine for the war with Russia because Ukrainian president Volodymyr Zelenskyy is Jewish. In practice they have done nothing to help Russia. Saudi Arabia has also tilted toward Moscow and has refused to expand oil production to keep oil prices from rising, which of course benefits the Saudi economy. The war has hurt Yemen, which depends on Russia and Ukraine for food.

Saudi Arabia and Iran have also begun to cool bilateral tensions. Iraq has hosted a half dozen meetings between the two and hopes to reach agreement to restore diplomatic relations broken by the Saudis in 2016. In early 2023 they promised to restore relations in a meeting convoked by China.

BIDEN'S TRIP TO JIDDA

In July 2022 President Biden abandoned his policy of isolating Muhammad bin Salman and traveled to Jidda, where he famously did a fist bump with the crown prince. He also attended a summit of the Gulf Cooperation Council states plus Egypt, Jordan, and Iraq. There were no major announcements from the visit, but the Saudis were eager to trumpet the return of the American president to the Kingdom and the rehabilitation of MBS.

The president's advisers had convinced the reluctant president that the Russian invasion of Ukraine and the subsequent sharp increase in oil prices required a rapprochement with the crown prince. The Saudis did not increase oil production, however, and remained in close contact with Moscow. It was an unnecessary and ineffective visit. Then in October the Saudis actually reduced production. Biden was humiliated.

Fortunately, although the truce in Yemen was not extended again, the two sides adhered to its terms. Commercial flights continued, and the blockade was eased but not entirely lifted. Fighting was sporadic and did not threaten to return to full-scale war. But the truce is tenuous and could collapse at any time.

WHAT SHOULD WE DO?

No single policy is likely to bring peace to Yemen. In the end, that is up to the Yemenis, not the Americans and surely not the Saudis. Yemen is a very divided society today; whether it will ever be a unified state again is unclear. Ali Abdallah Saleh may be the only Yemeni to ever rule over a united Yemen. It may be wise for the international community to set its sights and goals on encouraging peace between the parts of Yemen, not on unification itself.

The place to start is in the UN Security Council. Yemen needs a new UNSCR to guide the peace effort, not one tilted deliberately toward Saudi interests. As a first principle that resolution should call for an immediate and total halt to all foreign interference in Yemen. This would mean ending the Saudi blockade of and airstrikes inside Yemen. All military support to the Hadi government should be completely halted.

This would also mean that Iran and its allies should halt their support to the Houthis, including ending the transmission of technical expertise for drones and missiles. Iranian and Hezbollah advisers would have to leave Yemen. But commercial air flights between Sana'a and Tehran should be allowed as well as Iranian development projects, including in the ports of Aden and Hudaydah.

The existing United Nations Verification and Inspections Mechanism (UNVIM) for Yemen should be greatly expanded in mission and personnel to provide inspectors at all Yemeni ports and airfields to ensure no major violations of the resolution are perpetrated by either side. The existing UNVIM mandate is tied to Resolution 2216 and involves inspecting only Houthi-controlled ports like Hudaydah.

If Saudi Arabia resumes military operations in Yemen and the full blockade, the United States should cease all arms sales and contracts with the Kingdom. All American military personnel should be withdrawn from the country, as should all American contractors, as was done in Afghanistan. This would include technicians keeping the Royal Saudi Air Force's fleet of American-produced aircraft operating and bombing Yemen.

The impact on the Saudi military would be immediate and devastating. The Royal Saudi Air Force would not be able to keep aircraft in the air, let alone operational fighting machines. The Saudi army and national guard would also be crippled. The navy would be the least impacted because it has a more diverse number of sources for its warships, but it too would be in difficulty.

Some have suggested that the Saudis would turn to Russia or China for military equipment. In reality the Saudis need American spare parts and equipment; Russian or Chinese matériel would be useless. If the United Kingdom joined Washington in pressing Riyadh, the impact would be even more austere for the Saudi military.

The United States can continue robust counterterrorism missions from bases elsewhere in the region, including Djibouti and Oman. The AQAP threat can be further reduced.

The tragedy of America's relations with the Yemens is now catastrophic. Two American presidents supported a deadly Saudi-led war to defeat the Houthis. The Houthis are indeed virulently anti-American, but they have actually done little if any harm to American interests. Instead, the Saudi war has made them the patriotic defenders of a small country fighting a rich neighbor backed by Washington and much of the Western world. It is time to bring this tragedy to an end. To his credit Biden has made it a priority and achieved some success.

Dealing with the Houthis will not be easy after the war. Their anti-American posture is deeply rooted in the origins of the movement. It is a lingering aftereffect of the bad decision to invade Iraq in 2003, now compounded by six years of support for a war led by a neighbor most Yemenis hate. Air strikes, blockade, and intentional mass starvation are the characteristics of a war three presidents have supported.

Nonetheless the Houthis have created a functioning government in the area they control, which includes representatives of other groups. Prime Minister Abdel Aziz bin Habtour is from the south and was Hadi's governor of Aden in 2014 and 2015. Foreign Minister Hisham Sharaf was in several governments starting in 2011. Neither is Houthi. The population of Sana'a has grown substantially to seven million people from fewer than three million in 2019 and two million in 2010 due to the relative security and food safety in the capital thanks to the Houthis.[15] The Houthis and their allies have also continued to live up to the Stockholm Agreement for Hudaydah.

We have lived with other countries with virulently anti-American policies in the Middle East for decades. Unlike Hezbollah and Iran, moreover, the Houthis have not carried out acts of violence against American interests outside Yemen. It will not be a friendly relationship, but it does not need to be violently hostile.

The urgent imperative is to halt the blockade entirely and get aid to the Yemeni people. That should be America's priority.

NOTES

CHAPTER 1

1. Eugene Rogan, *The Fall of the Ottomans* (New York: Basic Books, 2015), 226.

2. Rogan, *The Fall of the Ottomans*, 227.

3. Richard Sanger, *The Arabian Peninsula* (Ithaca, NY: Cornell University Press, 1954), 203.

4. Asha Mehra, "The Italo-Wahabi Sweep of South Western Arabia (1924–1927): The Dual Challenge of British Hegemony," *Proceedings of the Indian History Congress* 50, Golden Jubilee Session (1989): 780–84.

5. Sanger, *The Arabian Peninsula*, 204.

6. Bruce Riedel, "Oman: First Arab Leader to Washington in 1938, and Due for Another Visit," *Order from Chaos*, Brookings Institution, April 14, 2021.

7. Sanger, *The Arabian Peninsula*, 246–47.

8. Thomas W. Lippman, *Arabian Knight: Colonel Bill Eddy USMC and the Rise of American Power in the Middle East* (St. Vista, CA: Selwa Press, 2008), 187.

9. Lippman, *Arabian Knight*, 189.

10. Sanger, *The Arabian Peninsula*, 260–62.

11. Sanger, *The Arabian Peninsula*, 267.

12. Lippman, *Arabian Knight*, 184.

13. "Operation Magic Carpet," Alaska Airlines, www.alaskaair.com/content/about-us/history/magic-carpet.

14. Bruce Riedel, *Beirut 1958: How America's Wars in the Middle East Began* (Washington, DC: Brookings Institution, 2020).

15. The best account of the Yemen war is Jesse Ferris, *Nasser's Gamble: How Intervention in Yemen Caused the Six-Day War and the Decline of Egyptian Power* (Princeton, NJ: Princeton University Press, 2015).

16. Parker T. Hart, *Saudi Arabia and the United States: Birth of a Security Partnership* (Bloomington: Indiana University Press, 1998), 114.

17. See also Bruce Riedel, *Kings and Presidents: Saudi Arabia and the United States since FDR* (Washington, DC: Brookings Institution Press, 2017).

18. Hart, *Saudi Arabia*, 243.

19. Tony Geraghty, *Soldiers of Fortune: A History of the Mercenary in Modern Warfare* (New York: Pegasus, 2009), 86.

20. Riedel, *Kings*, 42. See also Duff Hart-Davis, *The War That Never Was: The True Story of the Men Who Fought Britain's Most Secret Battle* (London: Random House, 2011); Ronen Bergman, "The Officer Who Saw Behind the Top-Secret Curtain," *Ynetnews Magazine*, June 22, 2015, www.ynetnews.com/articles/0 ,7340,L-4671127,00.html; author interviews with Nahum Admoni and Yossi Alpher.

21. Geraghty, *Soldiers*, 98.

22. Hart, *Saudi Arabia*, 193.

23. Yossi Alpher, *Periphery: Israel's Search for Middle East Allies* (London: Roman & Littlefield, 2015), 37.

24. Bergman, "The Officer Who Saw Behind the Top-Secret Curtain"; interviews with Alpher.

25. Victoria Clark, *Yemen: Dancing on the Heads of Snakes* (New Haven, CT: Yale University Press, 2010), 100.

26. Nick van der Bijl, *British Military Operations in Aden and Fadfan* (Croydon, UK: Pen and Sword Books, 2014), 200.

27. Kai Bird, *The Good Spy: The Life and Death of Robert Ames* (New York: Random House, 2014), 51–71.

CHAPTER 2

1. Memorandum from Secretary of State Kissinger to President Ford, Washington, DC, January 9, 1975, *Foreign Relations of the United States, 1969–1976*, Vol. E-9, Pt. 2, Documents on the Middle East Region, 1973–1976.

2. Memorandum of Conversation, Visit of Sultan Qaboos to the Oval Office, January 9, 1975, White House, Washington, DC, Ford Library Museum document 0314.

3. Victoria Clark, *Yemen: Dancing on the Heads of Snakes* (New Haven, CT: Yale University Press, 2010), 75.

4. Reuters, "Abdallah al-Salal Dies in Yemen at 74; Led 1962 Uprising," *New York Times*, March 6, 1994.

5. "Yemen: The Last Lunch," video posted to YouTube by Al Jazeera English, January 29, 2020, https://www.youtube.com/watch?v=1dsGeHxzzW8.

6. Jim Hoagl and Dan Morgan, "U.S. Speeds Arms for N. Yemen," *Washington Post*, March 7, 1969; Jim Hoagl, "Taiwanese Hired by North Yemen to Fly U.S. Jets," *Washington Post*, May 28, 1979.

7. Kambiz Fattahi, "The Oman Scare: The Untold Story of Oman's 'Almost Military Strike' on Iran," *Sources and Methods*, Wilson Center, September 27, 2018, https://www.wilsoncenter.org/blog-post/the-oman-scare-the-untold -story-omans-almost-military-strike-iran.

8. Jeffrey Engel, *When the World Seemed New: George H. W. Bush and the End of the Cold War* (Boston: Houghton Mifflin Harcourt, 2018), 379.

9. Dusko Doder, "Soviets. N. Yemen, Sign Treaty," *Washington Post*, October 10, 1984.

10. Jonathan Alter, *His Very Best: Jimmy Carter, a Life* (New York: Simon & Shuster, 2020), 665.

11. Clark, *Yemen*, 159.

12. Clark, *Yemen*, 160.

13. Timothy McNulty, "Bush Elated by North Yemeni Crowds," *Chicago Tribune*, April 12, 1986.

14. Memorandum of Conversation, Subject: Private Meeting with President Saleh of Yemen, January 24, 1990, White House, available in the George Bush Library.

15. Clark, *Yemen*, 132.

16. Robert Hurd and Greg Noakes, "North and South Yemen: Lead Up to the Breakup," *Washington Report of Middle East Affairs* (July/August 1994): 48.

17. James Blight et al., *Becoming Enemies: U.S.-Iran Relations and the Iran-Iraq War, 1979–1988* (Lanham, MD: Rowman & Littlefield, 2012), ix.

18. George Bush and Brent Scowcroft, *A World Transformed* (New York: Alfred A. Knopf, 1998), 314.

19. Engel, *When the World Seemed New*, 409.

20. Clark, *Yemen*, 156.

21. Clark, *Yemen*, 143.

CHAPTER 3

1. Edmund Hull, *High-Value Target: Countering Al Qaeda in Yemen* (Washington, DC: Potomac Books, 2011), 25.

2. Bill Clinton, *My Life* (New York: Knopf, 2004), 925.

3. Ali Soufan, *The Black Banners Declassified* (New York: Norton, 2020), 201.

4. George Tenet, *At the Center of the Storm: My Years at the CIA* (New York: Harper Collins, 2007), 128.

5. Victoria Clark, *Yemen: Dancing on the Heads of Snakes* (New Haven, CT: Yale University Press, 2010), 174.

6. Clark, *Yemen*, 171.

7. Clark, *Yemen*, 223.

8. Clark, *Yemen*, 201.

9. Clark, *Yemen*, 195.

10. Hull, *High-Value Target*, 25.

11. Andrew McGregor, ed., *Yemen and the United States: Different Approaches to the War on Terrorism, the Battle for Yemen* (Washington, DC: Jamestown Foundation, 2010), 209.

12. McGregor, *Yemen and the United States*, 208.

13. Shaun Overton, "Understanding the Second Houthi Rebellion in Yemen," in McGregor, *Yemen and the United States*, 169.

14. Clark, *Yemen*, 256.

15. Dexter Filkins, "After the Uprising," *New Yorker*, April 4, 2011.

16. Ben Hubbard, *MBS: The Rise to Power of Mohammed bin Salman* (New York: Tim Duggan Books, 2020), 90.

CHAPTER 4

1. Ben Hubbard, *MBS: The Rise to Power of Mohammed bin Salman* (New York: Tim Duggan Books, 2020), 91.

2. John Brennan, *Undaunted: My Fight against America's Enemies at Home and Abroad* (New York: Insightful Books, 2020), 339.

3. Hubbard, *MBS*, 91.

4. Bruce Riedel, *What We Won: America's Secret War in Afghanistan, 1979–89* (Washington, DC: Brookings Institution Press, 2014), 61.

5. Author conversations with Nawaz Sharif and his aides, spring 2015.

6. Associated Press, "Barack Obama Heads to Saudi Arabia to Pay Respects and Meet New King: Vice President Joe Biden Originally Was to Visit," *Guardian*, January 24, 2015.

7. John Tirman, Hussein Banai, and Malcolm Byrne, *Republics of Myth: National Narratives and the US-Iran Conflict* (Baltimore: John Hopkins University Press, 2021), 266.

8. Robert Malley and Stephen Pomper, "Yemen Cannot Afford to Wait," *The Atlantic*, April 5, 2019.

9. Barbara Slavin, "US Maintains Intelligence Relationship with Houthis," *Al Monitor*, January 21, 2015.

10. Author interview with Joseph Westphal, March 4, 2021.

11. Samantha Powers, *The Education of an Idealist: A Memoir* (New York: Harper Collins, 2019).

12. Susan Rice, *Tough Love: My Story of the Things Worth Fighting For* (New York: Simon & Shuster, 2019), 450.

13. John Kerry, *Every Day Is Extra* (New York: Simon & Shuster, 2018), 485.

14. Wendy R. Sherman, *Not for the Faint of Heart: Lessons in Courage, Power and Persistence* (New York: Public Affairs, 2018).

CHAPTER 5

1. Ben Hubbard, *MBS: The Rise to Power of Mohammed bin Salman* (New York: Tim Duggan Books, 2020), 106.

2. Hubbard, *MBS*, 114.

3. Hubbard, *MBS*, 119.

4. "The Young and Brash Saudi Crown Prince," *New York Times*, June 23, 2017.

5. Jamestown Foundation, *The Battle for Yemen* (Washington, DC: Jamestown Foundation, 2010), 147.

6. "Snakebitten: Ali Abdallah Saleh's Death Will Shake Up the War in Yemen," *The Economist*, December 4, 2017.

7. Jamal Khashoggi, "With Ali Abdallah's Death Saudi Arabia Is Paying the Price for Betraying the Arab Spring," *Washington Post*, December 5, 2017.

8. Jamal Khashoggi, "Saudi Arabia's Crown Prince Must Restore Dignity to His Country—by Ending Yemen's Cruel war," *Washington Post*, September 11, 2018.

9. Omer Karasapan, "Yemen and Covid-19: The Pandemic Exacts Its Devastating Toll," Brookings Institution, June 15, 2020.

10. Emma Farge, "Child Labour, Marriages on Rise in Yemen as Covid Spreads: UN Agency," *Reuters*, May 26, 2020.

CHAPTER 6

1. Robert Gates, *Duty: Memoirs of a Secretary at War* (New York: Knopf, 2014), 288.

2. Alex Emmons, "Joe Biden, in Departure from Obama Policy, Says He Would Make Saudi Arabia a 'Pariah,'" *The Intercept*, November 21, 2019.

3. Lyse Doucet, "Yemen War: Joe Biden Ends Support for Operations in Foreign Policy Reset," *BBC News*, February 4, 2012.

4. David Ottaway, "Biden's Peacemaking Bid in Yemen Faces Hard Truths," Wilson Center, March 23, 2021.

5. Maziar Motamedi, "Iran's Top Diplomat in Yemen Dies of Covid-19," *Al Jazeera*, December 21, 2021.

6. "U.S. Navy Says Large Weapons Shipment from Iran to Yemen's Houthi Rebels Seized from 'Stateless' Ship," *CBS News*, December 21, 2021.

7. Charles Pierson, "Smearing the Movement for Peace in Yemen," *Counterpunch*, November 5, 2021.

8. "UNDP: Recovery in Yemen Possible Despite Fast-Deteriorating Situation," United Nations News Centre, November 23, 2021; "Yemen War Deaths Will Reach 377,000 by End of the Year: UN," *Al Jazeera*, November 23, 2021.

9. Stephanie Kirchgaessner and Bethan McKernan, "Biden's $500 Million Saudi Deal Contradicts Policy on Offensive Weapons, Critics Say," *The Guardian*, October 27, 2021.

10. Brian Perking, "Saudi Arabia and the UAE in Al Mahra: Securing Interests, Disrupting Local Order and Shaping a Southern Military," *Terrorism Monitor*, Jamestown Foundation, March 1, 2019.

11. "Yemen: Saudi Forces Torture, 'Disappear,' Yemenis," Human Rights Watch, March 25, 2020.

12. Associated Press, "Mysterious Airbase Being Built on Volcanic Island off Yemen," *The Guardian*, May 25, 2012.

13. "Israeli Tourists Flock to Socotra: Part of Illegal UAE-Run Holidays," *Middle East Monitor*, May 19, 2021.

14. "Houthi Government Slams UAE over Israeli Tourists on Socotra and Airbase on Mayun Island," *Middle East Monitor*, June 2, 2021.

15. Aisha Jumaan, "Deconstructing the Saudi Narrative on the War in Yemen," *Responsible Statecraft*, January 12, 2022.

INDEX

Iran, 19–20; Contra, 24;
Houthis assisted by, 57;
JCPOA countering threat
of, 50; Obama preventing
nuclear weapons in, 43;
as root of evil, 56; shah
toppled in, 23; Trump
attacking nuclear agreement
with, 53; Yemen meddling
by, 51–52; Yemen war
profile increased by, 65
Iranian imperial troops, 19
Iranian Revolution, 46–47
Iran-Iraq War, 24–25
Iraq: cease-fire sought by,
22–23; Iran's War with,
24–25; Kuwait invaded
by, 27–28; Saleh, Ali,
background with, 27–28;
U.S. invasion of, 37; Yemen's
support for, 23–24, 28
Irlo, Hassan, 65
Ismail, Abd al-Fattah, 15,
20, 23
Israel: Arab's conflict with,
6, 17, 29, 32; clandestine
campaign by, 11; Egypt's
peace deal with, 22–23;
Mossad intelligence service
in, 11; Palestinian's peace
talks with, 34

JCPOA. *See* Joint
Comprehensive Plan of
Action
Jidda trip, 71–72
Johnson, Lyndon, 13
Joint Comprehensive Plan of
Action (JCPOA), 48–50, 65

Kennedy, John F., 6–8; civil
war warning to, 9; Saudi
modernization and, 10;
Saudis getting aircraft from,
12; Yemen crisis handled by,
12–13; Yemen war avoided
by, 11
Kerry, John, 50–51, 67
Khashoggi, Jamal, 58–61,
63, 67
Khomeini, Ayatollah
Ruhollah, 23
Khrushchev, Nikita, 8, 11
Kissinger, Henry, 17, 18
Kuwait, 22; agreement, 23;
Iraq invading, 27–28;
liberation of, 28–29, 44

Lenderking, Tim, 64

Macron, Emmanuel, 67
Al Mahra province, 57, 68–69
Malley, Robert, 65
Marco Polo, 1
Marlborough, USS, 34
Mattis, James, 60

About the Author

Bruce Riedel is a Senior Fellow in the Foreign Policy Studies program at the Brookings Institution where he specializes in the Middle East and South Asia. His previous books include *Kings and Presidents: Saudi Arabia and the United States Since FDR*, *Beirut 1958: How America's Wars in the Middle East Began*, and *Jordan and America: An Enduring Friendship*.

Ingram Content Group UK Ltd.
Milton Keynes UK
UKHW011337270723
425892UK00007B/51

9 780815 740131